Foreword by Dr. Luis Palau

Naked & Unashamed
RECAPTURING FAMILY INTIMACY

Bill Mills

BOOKS BY LEADERSHIP RESOURCES

Connecting With One Another Series

These devotional Bible studies are designed for personal growth as well as classes and small groups. Each book contains a 9-week discussion guide.

The Path of Joy: Enjoying Intimacy with God
by Marnie Carlson

Friendly Fire: Why Is God Shooting at Me?
by William G. Johnson

Changed: Experiencing God's Transforming Power
(Also available in Chinese)
by Bill Mills

Naked & Unashamed: Recapturing Family Intimacy
(Also available in Spanish and Chinese)
by Bill Mills

A Quiet Heart: Discovering Peace & Power at Jesus' Feet
by Carla Jividen Peer

Beyond Independence: Reclaiming Our Life Together in Christ
by Bill Mills

Pursuing God: Finding Our Fullness in Christ
(Also available in Chinese)
by Bill Mills

Shoulder to Shoulder: How God Builds Spiritual Men
(Also available in Chinese)
by Bill Mills

The Day of the Lord! Preparing to Meet the Bridegroom
by Bill Mills

The Blessing of Benjamin:
Living in the Power of Your Father's Approval
by Bill Mills and Peter Luisi-Mills

Connecting With God for Growth and Ministries Series

These devotional Bible studies will help you grow in your relationship with the Lord and in your ministry.

Adequate! How God Empowers Ordinary People to Serve
(Also available in Chinese)
by Bill Mills

Language of the Heart: Knowing Joy and Communion in Prayer
by Bill Mills

Finishing Well in Life and Ministry:
God's Protection from Burnout
(Also available in Spanish and Chinese)
by Bill Mills and Craig Parro

Unlikely Warriors: Our Call to Invade the Darkness
by Craig Parro

Inductive Bible Study Series

These Bible study helps will enable you to grow in your understanding of the Scriptures and in your preparation for teaching.

Proverbs: Lessons for the Growing Years (for Jr/Sr High)

Jonah: Inductive Bible Study

Philippians: A Family Bible Study

Ruth: The Romance of Redemption

Inductive Bible Study Handbook
by Dennis Fledderjohann

A Servant Series

Each book contains 21 articles from many well-known authors. Great library resources!

Marriage, Parenting & Forgiveness

Reconciliation, Fellowship & the Grace of God

You may order our books on our web site:
www.LeadershipResources.org

.

Ninth Printing—2005

© LEADERSHIP RESOURCES INTERNATIONAL 1990
12575 S. Ridgeland, Palos Heights, IL 60463
708-489-0022

We gratefully acknowledge the contribution of Diane Ooms in
developing the "Study Guide" at the end of each chapter.

THIS MINISTRY IS DEDICATED TO

The Glory of God
The Honor of His Word
The Building Up of the Body of Christ

For this reason I bow my knees before the Father, from whom every family in heaven and on earth is named, that according to the riches of his glory he may grant you to be strengthened with power through his Spirit in your inner being, so that Christ may dwell in your hearts through faith—that you, being rooted and grounded in love, may have strength to comprehend with all the saints what is the breadth and length and height and depth, and to know the love of Christ that surpasses knowledge, that you may be filled with all the fullness of God.

Ephesians 3:14–19

Table of Contents

Foreword

One of the greatest needs today is for our families to be transformed by the heart of God. If the family has success at home, the church is strengthened and its ministry of being salt and light is fulfilled. That is God's ideal, but not always the reality. As I travel around the world, I see how Satan, the enemy of the souls, has deceived husbands and wives, making them believe that we do not need the presence, direction and power of the Spirit in our homes. Many deceive themselves into thinking that marital intimacy and joy can come through minimal effort, or by merely hearing but not practicing the Word of God.

However, today as always, we can depend upon the Bible as our guide for interpersonal and family relationships! When our marriage relationship grows cold, suspicions start, and with them resentments and bitterness. As we give room to Satan, we begin to lose the joy and peace in our hearts. We simply will not experience real joy nor peace if Christ does not reign sovereignly in our lives and in our relationships.

Since we are children of God, we don't have to hide—either from one another or from God. We don't need to live with masks. We can live with uncovered faces and with transparent relationships. We need not feel wounded for life, nor to allow our bitterness to take root and spill over into the world. God's children can cry out to Him for our families and receive from Him the answers we need. We can go to the Lord of the family. He made families for Himself, and only He can preserve them. He has graciously provided the answers in His eternal handbook, the Bible.

I give thanks to God for books like Naked & Unashamed, books that make clear that only the Word of God provides answers. In a time when quick, superficial remedies are dispensed, and when self-help formulas are hailed—containing well-intended but faultily-grounded principles—Naked & Unashamed emphasizes that only what God does lasts forever, and that only He can resolve the maladies and problems of men's hearts. Only He can forgive sin and restore people.

I praise God for Bill Mills, a servant with a pastor's heart, who goes to the Scriptures to find solid principles for the family today. How good it is to know God can do what men cannot do! He can reunite what is broken before the eyes of a watching world.

There is hope for your family, reader, to raise children for God in a rebellious world, for uniting husband and wife in one heart. The hope is in God.

Dear reader, bow your heart before the Lord and ask Him to work in your life. Perhaps past experiences have made you doubt the power of God; maybe you have been defrauded time and again; perhaps you are unable to believe that anyone or anything is able to perform the miracle you are waiting for. For more than three decades I have seen how God has changed lives, hearts, and entire families. I assure you it doesn't matter what your family looks like today. God can transform it. He can make the wife a real refuge for her husband's heart, and can make the husband a true servant for his wife and children. God specializes in the impossible!

I believe that the central message of *Naked & Unashamed* is the declaration that God has made everything for His glory and honor, that we cannot add or take away from what God does, and that He wants to be glorified in our lives and in the lives of our families. My prayer, then, is that God would move your heart in such a way that you will glorify Him, and that His Word and eternal plan will be fulfilled in your life.

May God prosper His will in you and may you delight in seeking God's heart for your family.

Luis Palau
International Evangelist
Portland, Oregon

Now to him who is able to do far more abundantly than all that we ask or think, according to the power at work within us, to him be glory in the church and in Christ Jesus throughout all generations, forever and ever. Amen.

Ephesians 3:20-21

Introduction

As the apostle Paul wrote to the Christians at Ephesus, his prayer revealed his own heart, and even the heart of God, for families.

> For this reason I bow my knees before the Father, from whom every family in heaven and on earth is named, (Ephesians 3:14-15)

In these days of great pressure and attack on the family unit, we need to be reminded that God supplies all that is needed for our families to be all that He has designed them to be. It is from God that every family receives its identity. By His choice it is named; by the strength of His Spirit it is sustained; by the riches' of His glory it is fulfilled.

> ...according to the riches of his glory he may grant you to be strengthened with power through his Spirit in your inner being, so that Christ may dwell in your hearts through faith (Ephesians 3:16-17)

God tells us that the key to our relationship with Him and

with one another is Christ living in our hearts through faith. It is His life within us that is the means by which God is able to work out all of His will and purpose in our families. It is by His Holy Spirit that we are strengthened and enabled to walk in His ways. When Christ lives in our hearts, we are rooted and grounded in love that opens to us an understanding of God and His kingdom—His thoughts, His ways, His vision and purposes. God's love, too, motivates and empowers us to be the people He has called us to be in relationship to one another.

> —that you, being rooted and grounded in love, may have strength to comprehend with all the saints what is the breadth and length and height and depth, and to know the love of Christ that surpasses knowledge, that you may be filled with all the fullness of God. (Ephesians 3:17-19)

Paul prays that we might know the "love of Christ that surpasses knowledge." Surely, knowledge alone will never bring us to the place that God desires us to be as people and as families. The key to a successful life together can never result from gaining as much information as possible on the subject and then closely following the direction it gives. The Person of God, the love He provides through His Son, and the empowering of His Spirit are the only means by which our deepest hungers and our greatest needs can be fulfilled. No insight can transform our marriages and families; only the heart of God that has come alive within us through His Son can bring eternal changes. Paul's prayer, that we may be filled up to all of the fullness of God, is what we must desire in our marriages and in our families! As God fills our lives and our relationships, we become like Him and begin to walk in His ways. In a world in which we seek formulas, methods and principles, God calls us to seek Him, to know Him, and to be filled with His life.

Now to him who is able to do far more abundantly than all that we ask or think, according to the power at work within us, to him be glory in the church and in Christ Jesus throughout all generations, forever and ever. Amen. (Ephesians 3:20-21)

As Paul closes this prayer for the church and for families, he gives us great reason for confidence and hope: God is able to fulfill within us and within our relationships that which is far beyond even our greatest dreams. Often we look at our marriages and our families, and we see Christ's love evidenced in our relationships by freedom, security, and responsiveness. But sometimes we see hurts, shallow relationships, competition, even walls that have been built that are too high to climb over. Because we often approach these times with a sense of guilt, failure and hopelessness, we give up because we can't change anything any more. This is when God comes to us and gives great hope, freedom and confidence!

It is God who can do what we cannot do! He is the one who provides the resources of His life in order that our lives and our relationships might be made right and filled to overflowing. God can bring freedom, fulfillment and ministry far beyond our greatest hopes and dreams. His power working in us brings us into a new world, a place in which we can see the dreams come true that we have had for our marriages and families, and even those things far beyond what we have dared to dream!

It is our prayer that this study of the Scriptures might be an encouragement to your heart and a part of God's building process in your life, your marriage and your family. May God be glorified in the way in which you give yourself, and the heart of God, to one another.

Then God said, "Let us make man in our image, after our likeness. And let them have dominion over the fish of the sea and over the birds of the heavens and over the livestock and over all the earth and over every creeping thing that creeps on the earth." So God created man in his own image, in the image of God he created him; male and female he created them.

Genesis 1:26-27

1
Fellow Heirs of the Grace of Life

We come to marriage with hopes, dreams, and expectations, forged by our own background and by the way we have responded to God, our society, and our own feelings. We need only look around us to see that because people have a variety of reasons for choosing marriage, they bring many different expectations with them into a marriage relationship.

OUR DREAMS FOR MARRIAGE

The western world has a very romantic view of life and marriage. Sometimes romance is the power that draws people into marriage and the glue that keeps them in the relationship. I remember meeting with a fellow who had married a beautiful young woman just one year earlier. After only eight months of marriage, they had separated as a result of the pain that had surfaced. When I encouraged him to go back to his wife, he responded, "Bill, you can't imagine what I have endured in this past year!"

I put my arm on his shoulder and said, "Please don't talk about endurance after eight months of marriage." Although *endurance* is a word best used to describe a lifetime of commitment, that is where his heart was. When his marriage was no longer giving him what he had hoped for, the only way he knew to handle it was to bail out. Romance without a high level of commitment brings many relationships to the point where the marriage vows no longer mean "till death do us part" but rather "till you no longer give me what I desire in this marriage."

Some have described our culture, in which romance is such a high priority, as one in which we take a pot "heated to the boiling point" at the time of marriage and allow it to cool off over a period of years. In other cultures, in which the basis for relationships is not romance, a "cold pot" is taken and allowed to warm slowly over the years as the love grows.

Others see marriage as an opportunity to build a new life free from past failures, a place to fulfill a shared destiny now that they have put off past hindrances or escaped the controlling influence of others. Often after just a short time these people realize that they are still the same people, and they begin to reproduce the same failures in this new relationship.

In the kind of world in which we live, marriage is often seen as a means of escape from a painful home situation. Some of us come from homes and childhood's characterized by pain. Inflicted at every point of failure, the pain was an ongoing reminder that we did not measure up to someone else's expectations, and the absence of any affirmation may have been our only life experiences. We may see marriage as a way out, and we vow that *our* family life will be different. Then one day we realize that we are the same people that we were and that we have begun to multiply the same hurt and pain in our own families.

So often our dreams for our marriages and families are

dashed against the realities of our present lives, and our hopes are drained away by a sense of continual failure.

We need to know that God has dreams for our marriages and for our families. Seeing God's perception of and vision for these relationships can be the beginning of building according to His design. He brings redemption to our choices and our relationships.

A Call to Redemption

Seek the LORD while he may be found; call upon him while he is near. (Isaiah 55:6)

The time to respond to the Lord is always when He is speaking to us. No man ever gets up one morning and says, "Today I will begin to be the husband my wife needs and the father my children need. I will start now to orient my priorities around my family." That initiative doesn't begin in his own heart. It begins in the heart of God. In the same way, no woman on her own initiative says, "Today I will begin to be the source of encouragement my husband needs. I will be a warm and sensitive mother to my children." That desire does not find its birth in her feelings but in the work of the Holy Spirit within her heart.

We do not meet God on our own timetables or according to our own personal agendas. The Bible repeats the following passage several times as a warning to God's people to respond to His voice:

For he is our God, and we are the people of his pasture, and the sheep of his hand. Today, if you hear his voice, do not harden your hearts, as at Meribah, as on the day at Massah in the wilderness. (Psalm 95:7-8)

God continues with His call for people to turn to Him:

Let the wicked forsake his way, and the unrighteous man his

thoughts; let him return to the LORD, that he may have compassion on him, and to our God, for he will abundantly pardon. (Isaiah 55:7)

This is a wonderful promise! Wherever we have been, whatever we have done, whatever have been our weaknesses and failures, we can always return to Him and be confident of the depth of His mercy and the abundance of His pardon.

OUR THOUGHTS AND GOD'S THOUGHTS

God sets before us a picture of the miraculous transformation He will fulfill in us by means of His Word and His Spirit as He builds into us His perspectives and His responses:

For my thoughts are not your thoughts, neither are your ways my ways, declares the LORD. For as the heavens are higher than the earth, so are my ways higher than your ways and my thoughts than your thoughts. (Isaiah 55:8-9)

God so desires His people to know that the thoughts that fill our minds are vastly different from those that fill His mind. Those things that come out of our lives are poles apart from those that pour forth from His heart and life. God invites us to exchange our thoughts for His thoughts and our ways for His ways. He will build His perspectives into our minds and His responses into our heart.

Nowhere in our relationships in this world is the need to know God's thoughts and share His ways greater than in marriage. It is the place in which we must learn to think from His perspective and respond consistently with His own heart. The world tells us to live our lives on the basis of what gives us pleasure, to remain with someone as long as the relationship is consistent with our own goals, to make key decisions on the basis of our own desires. *God* calls us to establish relationships of commitment and faithfulness and to give ourselves to one another unselfishly as He has given Himself to us.

GOD'S DREAMS FOR MARRIAGE

Right from the beginning, God gives us His thoughts and vision for the marriage relationship. On the sixth day of creation, God spoke into being the animals "according to their kinds." He was pleased with His creation and called it good:

> And God said, "Let the earth bring forth living creatures according to their kinds—livestock and creeping things and beasts of the earth according to their kinds." And it was so. And God made the beasts of the earth according to their kinds and the livestock according to their kinds, and everything that creeps on the ground according to its kind. And God saw that it was good. (Genesis 1:24-25)

After the creation of the animals we have the record of the creation of man, in which God's creation was again fulfilled according to His spoken word.

> Then God said, "Let us make man in our image, after our likeness. And let them have dominion over the fish of the sea and over the birds of the heavens and over the livestock and over all the earth and over every creeping thing that creeps on the earth." So God created man in his own image, in the image of God he created him; male and female he created them. (Genesis 1:26-27)

There were no animals before God created the animals "according to their kinds." Surely there was an image in the vast, eternally creative mind of God, a picture of what each animal should look like. As God spoke, each one appeared, perfectly consistent with that image. However, when God created man, He did not say, "Let them appear after *their* kind." He made man after His kind. God created us *in His own image.*

This is what gives us all of our value and potential; we are made in the image and likeness of God. Our intellect, our emotions, and our will are a reflection of His own. God has given us the ability to comprehend the eternal, to respond from our hearts, and to move with purpose. This is the basis for our relationship with God and with one another. We can know God and live responsively before Him because He has made us like Himself. We can share life intimately in responsive relationships with one another because we are made in the image of God.

We are able to live together in relationships of intimacy and life because God has made us in His image. When we experience that intimacy, we also reflect the relationship among the members of the Trinity, and the world and the angels who are watching can see the reality of God in us.

Immediately after God made us in His image, He commissioned us to rule, to have authority over the creation. We must understand the relationship between being made in the image of God and having authority. Our ability to rule our lives and to have a sense of authority in our relationships and in those areas of ministry God entrusts to us is a result of our being made in the image of God: To the degree that we grow in becoming more like God, our lives express the true authority that comes from Him.

We must also see ruling as a shared ministry. God did not commission Adam with the authority over creation and then tell Eve that she could try to add a bit here and there if she felt able. Theirs was a ministry of shared authority in God's creation.

A MINISTRY OF FRUITFULNESS

After God created Adam and Eve, He blessed them and commissioned them for ministry in His creation. He gave them a stewardship with eternal implications:

And God blessed them. And God said to them, "Be fruitful and multiply and fill the earth and subdue it and have dominion over the fish of the sea and over the birds of the heavens and over every living thing that moves on the earth." (Genesis 1:28)

Be fruitful, multiply, and fill the earth. We know that in one sense this refers to populating the earth and filling it with sons and daughters, but there is a larger sense in which Adam and Eve participated with the Person of God in filling the earth with all of the fruit of His life. God created Adam and Eve in His own image so that they would "image Him" before Himself, before His angels, before each other, and before the world. Then He placed them in that creation as His agents, vessels of the life that comes from Him. They were to fill the earth with the things that express the life of God, that is, with His glory. As they reflected all of the characteristics of the Person of God, they would become a means by which God's ultimate purpose for time and creation would come to pass:

> For the earth will be filled with the knowledge of the glory of the LORD as the waters cover the sea. (Habakkuk 2:14)

God called Adam and Eve not only to fill the earth but also to subdue it. Again, with a sense that Adam and Eve were working as His agents, God directed them to bring the earth into subjection, to cause it to be their servant, and to stimulate it to fruitfulness. He desired that they would relate to the earth in such a way that it would respond to their ministry, reflecting the fruitfulness that flows from the life of God. Adam and Eve were to cause all of the earth to bear the mark of God's glory.

After commanding Adam and Eve to rule within this realm, God gave them the bountiful provision of the Garden to sustain them. The plants would provide food not only for man but also for the animals. God looked at His creation again after the sixth day and called it good.

A STEWARDSHIP OF CULTIVATION

In Genesis 2, we have another record of the creation of man and his commission to ministry.

> These are the generations of the heavens and the earth when they were created, in the day that the LORD God made the earth and the heavens. When no bush of the field was yet in the land and no small plant of the field had yet sprung up—for the LORD God had not caused it to rain on the land, and there was no man to work the ground, and a mist was going up from the land and was watering the whole face of the ground— (Genesis 2:4-6)

As we look at this second account of the creation of man, we see quickly that God's first desire for man and his ministry was that of cultivating the ground. From the beginning of time, God has wanted us to see our purpose and ministry as that of co–workers with Him in the midst of His creation—cultivating it, stimulating it to fruitfulness.

> ...the LORD God formed the man of dust from the ground and breathed into his nostrils the breath of life, and the man became a living creature. And the LORD God planted a garden in Eden, in the east, and there he put the man whom he had formed. (Genesis 2:7-8)

When we read of the creation of the animals, we see a picture of them emerging out of the spoken Word of God exactly according to the perfect image in His mind. But with man, we see a clear and intimate picture. God took something of the earth, formed it, breathed His own life to fill it, and man became a living being! We alone share God's nature and His life in the midst of this world. Next, we see a description of the Garden with every tree pleasing to the sight, and two trees in the midst of the Garden.

> And out of the ground the LORD God made to spring up every tree

that is pleasant to the sight and good for food. The tree of life was in the midst of the garden, and the tree of the knowledge of good and evil. (Genesis 2:9)

After a further description of the great beauty and riches of the Garden of Eden, a picture is again given of the ministry that God had entrusted to man.

The LORD God took the man and put him in the garden of Eden to work it and keep it. (Genesis 2:15)

Can you visualize God placing Adam in that garden and instructing him to cultivate and keep it? What a ministry of discipleship that must have been—God personally teaching Adam how to cultivate the ground and produce fruit! Once again, we see the desire in God's heart for man to be His agent to stimulate the fruitfulness of His life in the midst of His creation.

After placing man in the Garden to cultivate and keep it, God warned him not to eat of the tree of the knowledge of good and evil. To disobey would bring certain death.

And the LORD God commanded the man, saying, "You may surely eat of every tree of the garden, but of the tree of the knowledge of good and evil you shall not eat, for in the day that you eat of it you shall surely die." (Genesis 2:16-17)

Adam and Eve did disobey God, and in eating from the tree of the knowledge of good and evil, they declared their independence from Him. They fell in their sin, and as God has said, they died that very day. The law of death came to reign upon all of creation because of their disobedience.

We have lost our ability to follow God's original call to cultivate His fruitfulness within His creation apart from His redemption. Now, as a result of the Fall, rather than stimulate the earth to reflect the glory of God, we cause the earth to reflect our own death. The air, the water, the ground, all of the environment in which we live have come to reflect the pollution of the sin within our hearts. Through the blood of Christ God has redeemed us, and He desires His redeeming life to flow through us to all of His creation in order that His glory might fill the earth.

A TOOL OF EVANGELISM

Even in our disobedience and death, we see God's great heart of evangelism. From the beginning of time His great desire has been for the earth to be filled with all that comes from Him: His image, His life, His glory. He called Adam and Eve, the first couple, to walk with Him in that ministry, and it is the shared ministry of a husband and wife today. God desires our response to this high calling in marriage. In the record of the creation, we see a picture of evangelism: Adam and Eve working together as God's agents to cultivate the fruitfulness of His own life within this world.

In the Scriptures, God uses marriage to describe His relationship with His people as a testimony to the world. In Isaiah 54, God calls Himself the husband of His people:

> For your Maker is your husband, the LORD of hosts is his name; and the Holy One of Israel is your Redeemer, the God of the whole earth he is called. (v. 5)

In Jeremiah 3, God tells His people that they have "played the harlot" in their relationship with Him by serving other gods:

> "If a man divorces his wife and she goes from him and becomes another man's wife, will he return to her? Would not that land be greatly polluted? You have played the whore with many lovers; and would you return to me?" declares the LORD. Lift up your eyes to the bare heights, and see! Where have you not been ravished? By the waysides you have sat awaiting lovers like an Arab in the wilderness. You have polluted the land with your vile whoredom. (vv. 1-2)

Through the prophet Hosea, God again pictures His relationship with His people as a marriage—a betrothal in faithfulness:

> And I will betroth you to me forever. I will betroth you to me in
> righteousness and in justice, in steadfast love and in mercy. I
> will betroth you to me in faithfulness. And you shall know the
> LORD. (Hosea 2:19-20)

The apostle Paul used marriage as a picture of Christ's relationship with His church (see Ephesians 5:22-33). We see a clear
pattern in the Scriptures that God desires our marriages to be
expressions of our relationship with Him. In fact, within the
church of Jesus Christ, our marriages might be one of the primary and most powerful evangelistic tools we have for communicating the life and love of God to the world around us. Where else
can the world look and see such clear pictures of commitment,
faithfulness, love that endures in the midst of failures, God's forgiveness, His compassionate, giving love being shared intimately? As God has called us to cultivate the fruitfulness of His
life in the midst of this world, to stimulate the realm in which we
live to bear the marks of His glory, our marriages are a primary
tool for that ministry. Our relationships with one another become mirrors that reflect the love of God to the world.

AN ETERNAL BATTLEGROUND

Our marriages are not only primary tools for communicating the
love of God to the world; they are also front-line targets of Satan's
attacks. We will look at Genesis 3 in detail in the next chapter,
but in this context we see a clear progression of Satan's method-
ology for destroying the Kingdom of God and the family unit. Here
we see him tempting Eve in order to set her against her husband
and get her to disobey God. In submitting to Satan, Eve manipu-
lated Adam to place his desire to please her above his desire to

obey the Lord. When Adam sinned, the intimacy and freedom of the marriage relationship were affected in a devastating way for all time.

Satan's attack against the family continued. When God gave Adam and Eve children, Cain yielded to sin and killed his brother, Abel, and things continued to go downhill from there. The apostle Paul traces the results of sin and rebellion against God. In man's twisted desire to glory in himself and reject everything that comes from God, he became totally depraved in every area of his life, including his relationships. The fruit of this degrading lifestyle was homosexuality:

> For this reason God gave them up to dishonorable passions. For their women exchanged natural relations for those that are contrary to nature; and the men likewise gave up natural relations with women and were consumed with passion for one another, men committing shameless acts with men and receiving in themselves the due penalty for their error. (Romans 1:26-27)

What we see taking place in our society today is Satan's continued onslaught against the family unit that God created to communicate His name, His glory, and His nature to the world. What we are witnessing in terms of casual sexual relationships, divorce, pornography, abortion, homosexuality, and superficial marriage relationships are not isolated incidents. They are all part of Satan's continuing plan to destroy the families that God has raised up to glorify His name. Satan wants to remove from us that ministry of "imaging God" before the world.

We must recognize that we are in the midst of an eternal war and that our family relationships are the front lines for this battle. When we look at our society today, we must admit we are not waging this war very effectively. In our own marriages, we need to see that when we struggle with selfishness, build walls of isolation from one another, lack forgiveness, and live according to wrong priorities, it is all part of the war that Satan is waging against what God desires to build for His glory. How we respond to one another at these times has eternal significance. We are either submitting to Satan's onslaughts against the family, or we are demonstrating God's character, nature, and love.

HOPE IN A NEW CREATION

When we look at God's thoughts for our marriage relationship, every one of us has a sense of not "measuring up." Who of us is adequate to fulfill this kind of ministry? Which one of us has not failed in our responsibilities to our partner or to our children? Only God, who can do "exceeding abundantly beyond all that we ask or think" can fulfill through us His ministry in the world.

Satan loves to hold before us the Scriptures that reveal God's design for marriage and family relationships and convince us that we are hopeless when it comes to meeting these expectations. He will tell us over and over that we have tried and failed, and he will seek to neutralize us in this battle by stealing away our hope.

Can God still use us to build families that glorify His name? What can give us hope when we are weak and prone to failure? God brought us hope when He revealed to Isaiah how He continues to create life in the midst of this world:

> "For as the rain and the snow come down from heaven and do not return there but water the earth, making it bring forth and sprout, giving seed to the sower and bread to the eater, so shall my word be that goes out from my mouth; it shall not return to me empty, but it shall accomplish that which I purpose, and shall succeed in the thing for which I sent it. (Isaiah 55:10-11)

Just as God created the world by His spoken word, He creates life within His people by the words He speaks. Satan reminds us of everything we are not, of how we have failed in the past, of the weakness of our relationships, and of our tendency to repeat those same failures again. When he tells us that we will never be any different, that our relationships will never change, God comes to us and brings hope. He is the One who can create life within us where there is no life now: in the deadness of our relationships, the deadness in our battles with temptation, the deadness we feel because of our failures.

Just as God brings new life to the earth as the rain and snow come down from heaven, by His Word and His Spirit He creates new life in individuals and families who respond to Him. We have hope because God is there and can change us by the power of His words.

A VISION FOR GENERATIONS

God takes a long-term view. His vision is for generations. When He calls families to Himself, it is His desire to raise up generations to praise His name. This is the inheritance we must pass on to our children:

> Give ear, O my people, to my teaching; incline your ears to the words of my mouth! I will open my mouth in a parable; I will utter dark sayings from of old, things that we have heard and known, that our fathers have told us. We will not hide them from their children, but tell to the coming generation the glorious deeds of the LORD, and his might, and the wonders that he has done. (Psalm 78:1-4)

God has called us to tell future generations the praises of the Lord and to speak of the wondrous works He has done. It is not only our immediate families who cultivate the world to stimulate the fruitfulness of God's life in this world; our children's children will be cultivating it as well:

[The Lord] established a testimony in Jacob and appointed a law in Israel, which he commanded our fathers to teach to their children, that the next generation might know them, the children yet unborn, and arise and tell them to their children, so that they should set their hope in God and not forget the works of God, but keep his commandments; and that they should not be like their fathers, a stubborn and rebellious generation, a generation whose heart was not steadfast, whose spirit was not faithful to God. (Psalm 78:5-8)

We live in a generation that has not prepared its heart before the Lord, a generation characterized by disobedience and rebellion. The ministry to which God has called us is that of preparing the hearts of a generation in order that they might be faithful to God. May God give us the grace to be faithful in this most significant stewardship.

GOD'S PURPOSE IS GOD'S GLORY

In the Scriptures God shows us a beautiful picture, filled with hope and redemption. He calls us to seek Him, gives us the fullness of His mercy and His pardon, invites us to exchange our thoughts for His, and then builds into us the responses His heart desires. After transforming us by the power of Christ's life, God once again entrusts to us the stewardship of stimulating His creation to fruitfulness, of "imaging Him," of being vessels through which He will pour His life into this world and fill it with His glory.

God does not bring people together in marriage primarily for our sakes; He brings them together primarily for *His* sake. His highest purpose for our marriages is not our happiness. Oh, He wants us to be happy, but He is concerned with bigger things than our happiness—His highest purpose for our marriages is His glory!

The ministry God gave to Adam and Eve is the same ministry

He gives to us in our marriages. He will fulfill it through us, even in our weaknesses and failures. God calls us to come to Him with our whole hearts, and then He fulfills all of His will in our lives. That is the measure of His grace!

GROUP STUDY GUIDE AND PERSONAL APPLICATION

1. Every couple comes to their wedding day with idealistic hopes and dreams. List some of the reasons people marry and how some of these reasons may lead to future difficulty.

2. God's Word and His Holy Spirit are able to transform our thoughts. Explain what Isaiah 55:8-9 is teaching us about our thinking and about how our thinking differs from God's?

3. What does shared authority in God's creation mean?

4. As part of their shared authority over creation, God gave Adam and Eve the ministry of parenthood. When He told them to "be fruitful and increase in number" (Genesis 1:28), what else did God have in mind besides population growth?

5. God desires that the whole earth be filled with His glory. Before whom did God wish Adam and Eve (and us today) to "image" Him?

6. How did man's fall affect his ability to subdue the earth as God had planned?

7. God created the earth and heavens, yet no plants appeared. There was no man to work the ground. How does God want us to see our purpose and ministry?

8. Explain how God's creation of man differed from His creation of the animals. What does this tell us about God's view of man?

9. Describe ways in which a Christian marriage can become an evangelistic tool before our watching world.

10. Our marriages are prime targets for Satan's continued onslaught. Read the progression of events in the Garden of Eden that ushered in devastation in the marriage relationship. Note the action verbs in each sentence of this progression.

11. Satan continues his attack on the family today. What are some of the ways in which Christian marriages struggle?

12. Describe how Satan seeks to steal our hope for change.

13. What is God's purpose for our marriages?

REFLECTIONS

God can use marriages and families to fill the earth with His glory. What steps can you take to cause your goals, attitudes, and relationships to be a reflection of God and His purposes? It is easy to put the pursuit of our own happiness above the pursuit of God's glory. Consider changes you can make today that will put God and His priorities first in your life.

Therefore a man shall leave his father and his mother and hold fast to his wife, and they shall become one flesh.

Genesis 2:24

2

Marriage As It Was—and Is

We are studying God's view of marriage—a relationship in which the fruitfulness of His life flows through us to one another, to our children, and to the world. God's design for us is that we operate as His agents, cultivating this world so that it is responsive to Him, stimulating the growth of fruit that will last for eternity. In this way God fulfills His purposes in our lives, and we become a means by which His glory will fill the earth.

A SUITABLE HELPER

As we continue to look at God's creation of the marriage relationship, we find a startling statement:

> Then the LORD God said, "It is not good that the man should be alone; I will make him a helper fit for him." (Genesis 2:18)

In the account of creation in Genesis 1, God looks over His creation again and again and calls it "good." We visualize His going through His creative process and nodding His head in approval each time. Now, for the first time, He is calling something *not* good: "It is not good for the man to be alone." In this record of the creation of marriage, God's first recorded thought is of Adam's need for companionship, for communion between him and a partner. In awareness of this need, God chooses to make a "helper suitable" for Adam.

Adam needs a helper? How often the words and ideas of the Scriptures stand in contrast to the culture in which we live. We do not often look at a man as being in need of a helper—except, of course, for "little things" like cooking and cleaning. Our society tends to feel that a man can usually take care of himself quite well. So many of us believe the world's images of a man with no real needs—the strong, silent type who can handle any situation, never at a loss, his emotions always in firm control. But a woman, by contrast, needs help! She needs protection and help with her emotions, with making decisions, with handling her money, and with fixing her car. We must make no mistake: When God instituted marriage, it was man who needed a helper!

In our culture the word *helper* is not highly esteemed. We think of one who has no real skills but is there to assist as the larger, more important tasks are handled by someone else. We picture a helper as one who does the "menial things" to make life easier for us. This is not the kind of helper God is describing in a wife. The word *helper* is one of the most exalted words in Scripture. God often refers to Himself as the helper of His people (Psalm 54:4; Isaiah 41:14). This, then, is a highly exalted ministry which the woman will fulfill in the life of her husband. She will bring to him the ministry of the Lord God:

> So out of the ground the LORD God formed every beast of the field and every bird of the heavens and brought them to the man to see what he would call them. And whatever the man called every living creature, that was its name. The man gave names to all

livestock and to the birds of the heavens and to every beast of the field. But for Adam there was not found a helper fit for him. (Genesis 2:19-20)

After God created the animals, He paraded them before Adam, and Adam named them. If we tend to visualize the first man as a creature possessing minimal intelligence, this Scripture passage will change that concept. Adam was a highly intelligent creature made in God's own image.

If you have ever taken a course in biology and had to memorize the names of the species of animals, you may remember how difficult that was. But Adam is not memorizing their names; he is giving them their names!

As we visualize this scene, we see God developing within Adam a sense of need. All of the animals have complements; they are male and female; they share a partnership with one another. As Adam has this growing need for a partner, he now sees that his partner cannot come from the animals; there is no "perfect complement." God will create one who corresponds perfectly to Adam's needs.

A Sanctuary for Adam's Heart

So the LORD God caused a deep sleep to fall upon the man, and while he slept took one of his ribs and closed up its place with flesh. And the rib that the LORD God had taken from the man he made into a woman and brought her to the man. (Genesis 2:21-22)

It is God who first saw Adam's need for a helper, and it is God who took the initiative to meet that need. After He put Adam to sleep, He took one of his ribs, fashioned it into a woman, and brought her to Adam.

It has been said that God did not take Eve from Adam's head

so that he would rule over her, or from his feet so that she would be his slave, but from his side so that they might walk together. There is some real truth in this. But what kind of picture is God giving to us by taking Eve from Adam's rib? Our ribs protect our vital organs. Our ribs protect our hearts. This would be Eve's ministry in the life of her husband—she would give protection to his heart!

Now we can understand more fully the kind of "suitable helper" Adam needed when God instituted the marriage relationship. Adam needed someone to protect his heart. When we look again at the image with which most men struggle in our world today, we have a real conflict. Not many men live with an understanding that their hearts need protection or that this is the ministry of the woman God has given to them. Too often men tend to withdraw quietly inside when they are struggling with their emotions, with failures on the job, or with their relationships. Not often enough is their first thought to run to their wife for encouragement, strength, and affirmation.

If a wife is to fulfill the ministry to her husband for which God created her, her husband must let her know his heart. He must share his feelings, his fears, his anxieties, his failures. Only then can his wife be the healing refuge God has designed her to be. What a vision God gives to a woman at the beginning of her marriage: She will become a sanctuary for the heart of her husband!

AN AFFIRMATION OF GOD'S CHOICE

Then the man said, "This at last is bone of my bones and flesh of my flesh; she shall be called Woman, because she was taken out of Man." (Genesis 2:23)

Adam responds to God's ministry in his life with great excitement; it is as if he says, "God, she is exactly what I need and desire!" Adam affirms God's choice of a partner for him, and he receives her with great joy. Often in our marriages today we think of those things we would like to change in our partners. Even if there is a basic love and acceptance, there are often physical, emotional, spiritual, and personality traits or habits that we would change if we had the opportunity. Sometimes we even communicate these things to our partners, either consciously or unconsciously, gradually developing in them a deep sense of insecurity, a feeling that they don't measure up to our expectations.

God has created each one of us with weaknesses. That is why, when God calls us to marriage, we are in need of a "suitable helper," a perfect complement, one who corresponds to our weaknesses. As we look at God's lifelong process of discipleship in our lives—the ministry of making us like Christ through the work of the Holy Spirit—our partners are often the primary tools He uses in that process. Sometimes what we see as weaknesses in our partners are just the areas God uses to build strength into us and into our relationship with one another. Like Adam we need to accept one another completely, with joy, and affirm God's choice of a partner for us. If we are not able to do this, our marriage relationship will remain shallow and insecure, bringing continual pain to our hearts.

If we focus on idealized hopes and dreams or live with unrealistic expectations of what the perfect marriage partner would be like and then continually compare our husbands and wives to the "ideal" we have created, we will never be free to affirm our partners as God's perfect choice for us. Only when we see God's sovereign hand in bringing us a "perfect complement" as He did for Adam, will we be able to experience joy and peace in God's choice. When we truly believe that our husbands or wives, even with their faults and weaknesses, are God's perfectly designed gifts to help us become all that we can be in Christ, we will be free to affirm our partner.

The ability to affirm one another grows out of our own sense of security and confidence. As our confidence in God's sovereign work in our lives grows, so does our freedom to communicate to our partners that they are God's gifts to us. God, then, uses this to give them a growing sense of security in their relationship with us. It is their knowing how we see them that deepens their freedom and confidence, and even the intimacy of our relationship. Otherwise, our partners would be continually living with the attitude, "I know my partner really wishes I were this or that," and the enemy would use that insecurity to steal away any growing intimacy between us.

I became a Christian when I was seventeen years old, just before my senior year of high school. In the middle of my senior year, God brought into my life the woman that I would marry some four and a half years later—a beautiful, red-haired girl with green eyes and a gorgeous smile! I was so immature as a person and as a Christian, and yet I had begun to dream that God would use me in ministry someday. What kind of woman should I marry if I was preparing for "the ministry?"

Not too many people have more images thrust upon them than the wives of ministers. Ministers' wives need the gifts of teaching, leading, and hospitality. They must be an excellent counselor and often, at least, have some ability to play the piano. As I was getting to know Karen, I realized that she did not have many of those gifts and abilities. As I search my heart deeply, in honesty I would also say that I did not believe that Karen was as mature as I was spiritually. Much of this I communicated to her, mostly in a nonverbal way.

But I had no idea what I needed in a wife. God has allowed me to go through times of sickness, times of great weakness and failure in my life and in my ministry. In all of this, the woman God gave me has been such a rock of stability for me, a great source of strength, a resource of the very life of God to me. Now I am able to look at her as Adam did when He first saw Eve and say, "God, she is exactly what I need!" Now I am able to affirm God's choice and to receive her with great joy. I only wish I could have done that from the very beginning of our life together.

As I grew in my own confidence of God's sovereign choices in my life, and as I saw the great beauty of God's gift to me in Karen, I grew also in my ability to affirm her as God's perfect gift to me. I told her again and again how I felt, and I let her see in my heart the wonderful joy I found in her. God used this to heal the insecurities of her own heart and to give her a growing sense of beauty, worth, and value. This became the environment in which God stimulated our love to growing depths of intimacy and joy.

UNION AND COMMUNION

Therefore a man shall leave his father and his mother and hold fast to his wife, and they shall become one flesh. (Genesis 2:24)

After God created Eve and brought her to Adam, He gave us the fullest, clearest summary statement on marriage in all of the Scriptures. This is how God sees marriage: For this cause (because God sees needs in the lives of His children and takes the initiative to meet those needs by bringing a man and woman to one another) a man shall leave, cleave (be united), and become one flesh with his wife. Let's look at each of these ideas a bit more.

Leaving: Commitment—the willingness to take responsibility in a relationship given by God—is always the beginning point of love. All former relationships must be submitted to this new relationship God is creating.

Cleaving: In this environment of commitment, a willingness to be vulnerable to one another begins to grow. The freedom to be known in order for the relationship to grow deeply begins to flourish. A thoughtful, willful opening of our lives to one another begins to take place between the partners. As we open our lives to one another, a giving/receiving/responding relationship develops in which the partners experience mutual growth and even healing with one another.

The partners who have committed their lives to one another now share a depth of intimacy and communion.

Becoming One Flesh: At the time of marriage, this new relationship is expressed in physical union. Built on the communion the couple already shares, physical union stimulates their relationship to even greater depths of personal intimacy. The sexual relationship becomes a physical, visible picture of the stimulation, encouragement, responsiveness, and shared joy that we need to express in every area of our lives together.

> And the man and his wife were both naked and were not ashamed. (Genesis 2:25)

Can you imagine a more beautiful way to describe a marriage relationship? Adam and Eve were naked and were not ashamed in one another's presence. This has to do with far more than their physical relationship. It is a picture of all of their life together. They were free to be seen in one another's presence as real people, with strengths and weaknesses, all of their person and their life exposed. They lived with great confidence in their marriage—they were vulnerable, open, wholly known, completely accepted, and affirmed. In God's design and provision they shared a deep intimacy and fulfillment in one another.

Here we see a picture of union and communion. Adam and Eve were both "in Adam" before God created their marriage relationship. There was union of life, but it was not possible for them to commune with one another. Then God took the rib from Adam's side and formed Eve and brought her to Adam. Now there was union of life again, but in such a way that there could be communion as well. As a result of God's creation of marriage, there can be both oneness and intimacy. That is God's desire for our lives together—union and communion.

THE BATTLE IN THE GARDEN

In Satan's desire to destroy the family God was building, he tempted Eve by causing her to speculate about what God had really said and to question it:

> Now the serpent was more crafty than any other beast of the field that the LORD God had made. He said to the woman, "Did God actually say, 'You shall not eat of any tree in the garden'?" (Genesis 3:1)

Satan came to Eve questioning God's words, even slandering them! He wanted Eve to speculate about the possibility that God might be withholding something that was good. Eve seemed to be sincere in her desire to do what was right but in her response, she added to what God had said.

> And the woman said to the serpent, "We may eat of the fruit of the trees in the garden, but God said, 'You shall not eat of the fruit of the tree that is in the midst of the garden, neither shall you touch it, lest you die.'" (Genesis 3:2-3)

God had never said anything to Eve about not *touching* the tree. In her battle against temptation, she placed her confidence in what she had added to the Word of God. ("If God said don't eat of the tree, then if I don't even touch it, I will really be safe.") This is the first record of legalism in the Scriptures. We do not need to add to what God has said. All we need to do is obey His Word.

Then Satan directly contradicted the Word of God:

But the serpent said to the woman, "You will not surely die. For God knows that when you eat of it your eyes will be opened, and you will be like God, knowing good and evil." (Genesis 3:4-5)

Satan came to Eve as the one who would reveal the mind of God to her. He told her that by submitting to him, Eve could grow to her fullest potential and even become like God, possessing the knowledge of everything evil and everything good:

So when the woman saw that the tree was good for food, and that it was a delight to the eyes, and that the tree was to be desired to make one wise, she took of its fruit and ate, and she also gave some to her husband who was with her, and he ate. (Genesis 3:6)

As Eve focused on the tree and speculated about Satan's temptation, the desire for the fruit of the tree grew within her. Finally, she took the fruit, ate it, and then gave it to Adam. He, too, ate the fruit. The Scriptures tell us that Eve was deceived but that Adam understood his actions and the implications of his disobedience:

...Adam was not deceived, but the woman was deceived and became a transgressor. (1 Timothy 2:14)

NAKED AND ASHAMED

Immediately after Adam and Eve sinned, the nature of their relationship changed. Before their sin, they were free to be "naked and not ashamed" in one another's presence. Now they responded to their nakedness by trying to cover themselves in each other's presence. No longer were they free to be seen physically, emotionally, intellectually, and spiritually as real people with strengths and weaknesses. As a result of their sin against God, they were free to reveal to one another only those things they were confident would be accepted; they hid from one another those areas they feared would be rejected. The loin coverings are a picture of the totality of their relationship with one another:

> Then the eyes of both were opened, and they knew that they were naked. And they sewed fig leaves together and made themselves loincloths. (Genesis 3:7)

God desires to restore our marriages to the state of freedom that Adam and Eve shared before the Fall—naked and not ashamed. The entry of sin into our human experience has drastically affected the dynamics of every relationship. Our responses to each other are tainted by Adam's fall, and only God can redeem us from shallow and superficial relationships.

We must know that the nature of sin will cause us to hide our lives from one another. Our natural tendency will not be openness with each other or the freedom to share our deepest feelings, hurts, or failures. Our first thought in difficult times will not be to share areas in which we are weak so that our partners can encourage us and pray for us. But we need to learn to live this way in the environment of God's redemption. We must be diligent, thoughtful, prayerful, sensitive, and compassionate as we cultivate this open, intimate, vulnerably responsive lifestyle with one another.

God is redeeming our relationships so that we can once again be naked and unashamed with one another. Because of sin, our marriage relationships, like that of Adam and Eve, have become deeply affected by guilt, shame, and fear. The guilt of our sin (our standing before a Holy God), our shame (our view of ourselves in light of our sin), and our fear of rejection, alienation, or punishment control our responses to God and to one another.

God deals with our guilt by clothing us in the righteousness of His Son when we receive Christ as our Lord and Savior. He covers our shame and then heals our hearts by teaching us to see ourselves through His eyes. He removes our fear by accepting us in His beloved Son, and now we cry, "Abba, Father" in His presence.

As we give to one another what God has given us in His Son, He brings that same redemption to our relationships. When we give to one another that same acceptance and forgiveness, and as we bear with one another and cover each other's sin with grace, God touches our relationships with His healing power. When we encourage each other to see ourselves through the eyes of God and bring to each other what God has brought to us through the death of His Son, guilt, fear, and shame no longer control us. Now the love of Christ controls our hearts and our responses, and in that environment we can be naked and not unashamed before Him and before each other.

GOD THE PURSUER

> And they heard the sound of the LORD God walking in the garden in the cool of the day, and the man and his wife hid themselves from the presence of the LORD God among the trees of the garden. But the LORD God called to the man and said to him, "Where are you?" And he said, "I heard the sound of you in the garden, and I was afraid, because I was naked, and I hid myself." (Genesis 3:8-10)

Adam and Eve hid not only from one another but also from God. When God came looking for them, they were hiding from Him among the trees of the Garden. Again we see so clearly that the nature of sin makes us withdraw, hide, and cover up in the presence of one another. That tendency is magnified many times over in the presence of a holy and righteous God. In Adam's response to God's call to come out of hiding, we see the devastating consequences of sin's taking root: "My guilt was exposed and I was filled with fear, and the only way I knew how to handle it was to hide." Fear, guilt, shame, and withdrawal are characteristic of the state of our lives and our relationships after the Fall. Our only hope is in a God who brings redemption in the midst of our sin:

> [The LORD God] said, "Who told you that you were naked? Have you eaten of the tree of which I commanded you not to eat?" The man said, "The woman whom you gave to be with me, she gave me fruit of the tree, and I ate." Then the LORD God said to the woman, "What is this that you have done?" The woman said, "The serpent deceived me, and I ate." (Genesis 3:11-13)

When God finds Adam and confronts him about his sin and disobedience, Adam refuses to take responsibility for his actions. He places the responsibility on Eve. There is even a sense that he holds God responsible. "The woman that you gave me," Adam tells God, "is the one who caused me to eat of the tree." Quickly we see the depth of depravity in Adam's heart. We can hear him saying to God, "If you had not given Eve to me, none of this would have happened." Adam is willing to hold the Lord God, the Holy One, responsible for his sins. That is how far and how quickly Adam has fallen in his sin.

Eve, likewise, refuses to take responsibility for her sin. She passes the responsibility on to Satan. Now God confronts Satan, Eve, and Adam with the curse and its effects in their lives and relationships:

> The LORD God said to the serpent, "Because you have done this, cursed are you above all livestock and above all beasts of the field; on your belly you shall go, and dust you shall eat all the days of your life. I will put enmity between you and the woman, and between your offspring and her offspring; he shall bruise your head, and you shall bruise his heel." (Genesis 3:14-15)

From now on the serpent, the "shining one" of incredible beauty and presence, will slither on his belly and eat dust. As God describes the enmity, hatred, and striving that will occur between the seed of the serpent and the seed of the woman, we find the Scriptures' first promise of the Redeemer. The seed of the serpent is Satan. The seed of the woman is the Lord Jesus. At the cross, Satan bruises Jesus' heel, but Jesus crushes Satan's head! Even before God confronts Adam and Eve with the fruit of their sin, the effects of the curse, He gives to them and to us a vision of redemption in a new covenant relationship with Him.

I do not know what this does to your heart, but it overwhelms mine. Adam and Eve have not repented of their sin, they have not confessed their sin, they have not admitted one iota of responsibility for their sin, and already God is talking about redemption! Any time we think that salvation is anything less than all of God, we are making a tremendous mistake. Redemption is what fills His heart; it is what He seeks; it is what He brings.

THE EFFECTS OF THE CURSE ON THE WOMAN

To the woman [God] said, "I will surely multiply your pain in childbearing; in pain you shall bring forth children. Your desire shall be for your husband, and he shall rule over you." (Genesis 3:16)

As God confronts Eve, He takes what has happened in her sin and disobedience and multiplies it in the effects of the curse. She had looked at that fruit on the tree of the knowledge of good and evil and believed Satan's lies that the fruit would be the means by which her life would be fulfilled. Now God applies the effects of the curse to the fruit of her life. In pain she will "bring forth" children.

We know that the physical process of giving birth is painful, but the picture here is much bigger: God is describing not only the difficult months of pregnancy or the painful hours of labor but the entire process of rearing children as well. All of this will be a source of pain in the life of a woman. Although this is by no means saying that children will not also bring great joy and happiness to their mothers, this lifelong ministry will be painful for her. She will identify intimately with every hurt, failure, and crisis in their lives in a way that is uniquely different from her husband's response. Every pain in their lives—falls, high fevers, school crises, dating problems, financial struggles, failure in relationships—will also bring increased pain to her heart.

Of course, this identification with the pain of her children will bring tension into her relationship with her husband because he will not readily understand why the children's every crisis, whether small or large, seems to captivate her in such a way. On many occasions she will tend to think that he doesn't care as much about the children as he should. He sometimes seems insensitive to their needs and may not appear to be a caring father because of his lack of involvement. These effects of the curse are reflected in their marriage relationship, and there is a continual need for redemption in their life together.

When our son Peter was in fifth grade, he was invited to be in the school spelling bee. He was so excited. Although I tried to communicate the value of being able to spell and handle words for his future success, he knew only that he wanted to be the best speller in the class.

I will never forget that day before Thanksgiving when Peter was to participate in the spelling bee. The school principal in his tall hat and the children in their pilgrim outfits were there. Peter had studied hard. We had prayed. He was ready!

There he stood in the middle of the thirty-five children. He had studied all of the hard words, but he was so nervous. When Peter's turn came, he stood, repeated the word *mittens*—and misspelled it! When the principal responded, "I'm sorry, Peter, that is wrong," the sense of failure and pain spread across his face. I will always remember looking at Karen, who sat next to me, and seeing the exact same expression on her face. It was all I could do to hold her down! She wanted to run over to our son, throw her arms around him and say, "It's okay, Peter. You really are a good speller. It will be all right. You will get through this and have successes in your life. It's okay, *I love you!*" Later Peter said, "If only it wasn't the first round; if only I wasn't the first one down in the whole class!"

The pain in Peter's heart was increased in the heart of his mother. That is what God is talking about in this Scripture passage. I know, too, that if I had been in Peter's grandmother's home that night when Karen called to give her the results of the spelling bee, I would have seen the same expression on her face. This is not something you outgrow. Those of us who have adult children living in great failure or in marriages filled with pain know what God is talking about here. I'm sure that we would give all of our material possessions as well as our very lives to heal the hearts of our hurting children. That is the effect of the curse: Every pain in the lives of a mother's children will be a great source of pain to her own heart. Something that was once good and beautiful—a mother's empathy for her children, her ability to intimately join her heart with theirs—has now become twisted in the effects of the curse. It has now become for her a point of great, sometimes debilitating, pain.

Here we must be reminded once again that we have a God who brings hope and redemption to us. There are different degrees of vulnerability among women from the effects of the curse. It helps us to understand why we struggle in these ways, but God is in no way condemning His children to a continual battle with no hope. Our redemption in Christ touches every area of our lives and our relationships. Through the comfort of our Father's mercies, the cleansing of the Scriptures, the resources of the Holy

Spirit, and the gentle love of a servant husband, God brings to every woman in Christ a way through these effects of the curse.

THE VULNERABILITY TO CONTROL

As God continues to confront Eve about the effects of the curse, He turns directly to her relationship with Adam. In the midst of the temptation, Eve was convinced she was doing the right thing. She looked at the fruit of the tree and truly believed that it would be a means of personal and spiritual growth. She took the initiative, grasped the fruit, ate it, and then gave some to Adam. Eve is controlling the situation and giving direction to Adam. This is the "desire" to which God is referring in the effects of the curse. As the fruits of sin are multiplied in Eve's life, she will have a desire to control her husband, to rule him, to manipulate him to build his life around her.

Once again something that is beautiful in the heart of a woman is being twisted in the effect of the curse. Her desire to encourage and support her husband, which is a wonderful and real source of ministry in his life, has now fallen to a tendency toward control and manipulation.

Although *control* is surely a strong word to use in this context, we see the same phrase in the original language in God's confrontation of Cain before he killed Abel. Sin was seeking to control him, but he must master it:

> If you do well, will you not be accepted? And if you do not do well, sin is crouching at the door. Its desire is for you, but you must rule over it. (Genesis 4:7)

Every woman is vulnerable to the temptation to manipulate her husband. She desires to be the center of his attention, his time, and all of his energy and affection. The tendency is always there to give direction to him and to their relationship together. It may come as a "mothering" attitude; it may be expressed in a competitive sense, but it will always create tension in the relationship. Since the Fall, every wife needs to be aware of this tendency, and every man needs God's wisdom and sensitivity to know when to give himself up for his wife to meet genuine needs and how to confront her lovingly in this process. In this way, he will be a part of God's redeeming ministry in the life of his wife and an expression of the hope that her Father brings.

THE EFFECTS OF THE CURSE IN THE MAN

Now God turns His attention to Adam, explaining the effects of the curse in his life:

> And to Adam he said, "Because you have listened to the voice of your wife and have eaten of the tree of which I commanded you, 'You shall not eat of it,' cursed is the ground because of you; in pain you shall eat of it all the days of your life; thorns and thistles it shall bring forth for you; and you shall eat the plants of the field. By the sweat of your face you shall eat bread, till you return to the ground, for out of it you were taken; for you are dust, and to dust you shall return." (Genesis 3:17-19)

The effects of the curse in the life of the woman apply to her relationship with her husband and her children, but for the man it applies to his relationship to work.

God begins His confrontation of Adam by saying, "Because you listened to the voice of your wife." Adam needs to understand the dynamics of their relationship in the midst of the temptation and sin. Eve believed she was doing the right thing; Adam knew it was sin. At this point in his life he made the choice to please his wife rather than to obey God. We must not misunderstand God's words to Adam. Surely there are many times when a man *must* listen to the voice of his wife. God will give counsel, help, comfort, and encouragement through her. Adam's problem was that he knew that what Eve wanted was wrong, but he did it anyway because he wanted to please his wife. He put his wife above God. That was his sin.

Now, because Adam has chosen to please his wife rather than God, the ground is cursed. Adam will toil continually and will look for the fruit the ground produces, but instead he will see thorns and thistles. What a source of frustration this toil will be! All of Adam's hopes for fulfillment will surface as he walks into the field and then will be disappointed because there will be so little fruit, so many thorns, and so much sweat expended in the process! The fruit of the tree of the knowledge of good and evil had been so easy to reach out and take. Now the fruit in the field that he desired so much would come only by the sweat of his brow.

We must see here the difference between "labor" and "toil." Work is a responsibility that God entrusts to us. *Work* existed before the Fall. *Toil* exists because of the curse. God gives us the freedom to enjoy our work, and King Solomon gave us clear instruction in this area.

> I perceived that there is nothing better for them than to be joyful and to do good as long as they live; also that everyone should eat and drink and take pleasure in all his toil—this is God's gift to man. (Ecclesiastes 3:12-13)

Some of us find great enjoyment in our work. There are times of real success and lasting results. However, we labor for the fruit of the ground that meets our daily needs. Every man is faced with the continual frustration of looking at his work as a means of fulfillment and instead sees thorns and thistles. There are time pressures, financial problems, difficulties in relationships, mechanical failures, and yet his hope for fruit and satisfaction from his work will always remain. He will repeatedly return to his field with this hope. Because of the curse, every man has this tendency to find his identity and fulfillment in his work. He spends his life working in the field of his choice, toiling with the sweat of his brow, and waiting in hope for the fruit to come.

The heart of every man is vulnerable to the temptation to become a workaholic. It is in our jobs—not primarily in our relationship with God or our ministry as a husband or a father—that we will tend to seek our identity and fulfillment. How often do we ask a man who he is and hear him respond by telling us what he does? Our hearts become so wrapped up in our work that we actually become what we do!

However, our hearts are not only *pulled* to our work because of the effects of the curse; they are also *pushed* to our jobs because of the economic pressures of the world in which we live. Many men are convinced that to provide a home for their families, an acceptable standard of living, and education for their children takes all of their time, their hearts, and their resources. In this way they tend to justify letting their jobs consume their lives and leaving the care of the children to their wives.

There is another aspect of this battle. It is often easier to be "successful" at work than it is at home. Many men who sincerely want to meet their wives' needs have great trouble discerning what they are. When they are confronted with the choices and temptations their children face every day, they tend to become overwhelmed. Not only are their hearts pulled to their work by the effects of the curse or pushed there by the economic pressures; a job can also become a wonderful place to "hide" when things aren't going well at home. It is one place in which a man can see the fruit of his labors quickly—even in the midst of the thorns and thistles—and have a sense of success and see the pieces fitting together properly.

Just as we saw with the woman, something that is right and

good in the heart of a man has become twisted in the effects of the curse. A man's desire and commitment to provide for his family are commendable in the eyes of God and in the society in which we live. But in the effects of the curse, a man may become so consumed with his work that he loses his life in his job. Only by the Spirit of God and the direction of His Word—and perhaps the counsel of his wife—will any man be able to maintain a proper perspective on the work God has entrusted to him.

To a great degree because of sin and the effects of the curse, men and women look at life from two completely different perspectives. Women tend to build their lives around their children and husbands while men tend to center their lives around their work. These tendencies result in misunderstandings, confusion, and very real hurts. The compassion and sensitivity that come only from God, as well as the communication He enables us to share at these times, will bring healing and redemption from the effects of the curse in our marriages and in our families.

A GOD WHO COVERS SIN

After Adam named Eve, we see God performing one of the most significant acts in all of history:

> The man called his wife's name Eve, because she was the mother of all living. And the LORD God made for Adam and for his wife garments of skins and clothed them. (Genesis 3:20-21)

It was God who shed the first blood in His creation. There must have been great pain and a sense of loss in His heart as He fulfilled this ministry. In the midst of Adam and Eve's guilt, fear, and shame, God took the initiative to cover their lives at the cost of precious life within His creation.

Adam needs to know that everything has changed because of his sin. Originally God had called him to eat freely of the tree of life, to draw his entire life from Him. Now, however, because Adam has chosen to no longer draw his life from God, other life in this world must continually be sacrificed in order for his own life to be maintained. In this world, we live at the expense of other life when we choose not to draw our life from God.

Because Adam and Eve could not adequately cover their lives with their insufficient loin coverings, God saw the real need and met it with the life that only He can give. What a picture this is of God's sending His own Son, redeeming us at the cost of Christ's blood, and covering our lives with His own righteousness.

> ...knowing that you were ransomed from the futile ways inherited from your forefathers, not with perishable things such as silver or gold, but with the precious blood of Christ, like that of a lamb without blemish or spot. (1 Peter 1:18-19)

GUARDING THE WAY TO THE TREE OF LIFE

We now see the further devastating consequences of Adam's and Eve's choices:

> Then the LORD God said, "Behold, the man has become like one of us in knowing good and evil. Now, lest he reach out his hand and take also of the tree of life and eat, and live forever—"therefore the LORD God sent him out from the garden of Eden to work the ground from which he was taken. (Genesis 3:22-23)

I don't think we can even begin to sense the anger and pain that must fill God's heart here. When we studied Genesis 1, we saw that God's highest vision and desire for man is that we should be like Him, made in His own image. Now God says, "The man has become like one of us in knowing good and evil."

What was it of God that we desired and pursued? Was it His holiness? His righteousness? His sense of justice? His mercy and compassion? No, the only thing of God that we have ever pursued in the flesh is to know everything that He knows. In our sin we become like Him in only one way—knowing good and evil.

In His wrath, God cast Adam and Eve out of the Garden of Eden. As a consequence of their sin, they are cut off from the tree of life. Sometimes God's greatest judgments take place in our lives when He gives us what we pursue. As a result, Adam and Eve will not draw their lives from God but from themselves and this world's resources.

But this is also an act of mercy: If Adam and Eve had eaten of the tree of life at this point in their lives, they would have lived forever in their sinful state. We must learn to see death, too, as a gift of God.

> He drove out the man, and at the east of the garden of Eden he placed the cherubim and a flaming sword that turned every way to guard the way to the tree of life. (Genesis 3:24)

The cherubim and the flaming sword guarded the way to the tree of life. Although we know that in one sense God is keeping Adam and Eve from the tree, so that they do not eat now and live forever in a sinful state, perhaps in another sense we can see the angels and the flaming sword guarding the way *to* the tree.

After sin, disobedience and death have entered the history of man, there is only one way back to God, to the place where He gives life. This way can never be found in the religions that we create or in our human efforts to be good people. Just as He was in the beginning of time, God is still the only way back to Himself. The cross at Calvary, where God's Son poured out His life and paid the price for our redemption, is the only back way to God. Throughout all of history, God has guarded the way to the tree of life; that way is His own Son:

> Jesus said to him, "I am the way, and the truth, and the life. No one comes to the Father except through me." (John 14:6)

GOD IS A GOD OF HOPE!

In Genesis 3 we find the darkest day in the history of mankind. Man—who was created in God's image, called as His co-worker in cultivating this realm to fruitfulness, and designed as a vessel for the ministry of God's life—rejected God and chose self-development instead. Relationships that once overflowed with life are now consumed with death. The results of this disobedience are sin and death, inherited from generation to generation. However, in contrast to the darkness of man's failure, there is a picture of the Person of God—His heart full of redemption.

When Adam was hiding in his guilt and fear, God sought him; in the midst of the curse, God promised redemption. When our own efforts to cover our lives proved utterly inadequate, God covered us with the life that can come only from Him. When we were cut off from the tree of life, God guarded the way back to Himself.

Some years ago our family visited Chicago's Museum of Science and Industry, where I was captivated by a photography exhibit. The focus was laser photography that results in a hologram. Although I hardly even began to understand what was being presented there, I do remember this graphic illustration: If we take a regular picture and tear the negative into pieces, every piece would contain part of the picture. In laser photography that results in a hologram, if we tear the negative into pieces, every piece would contain the whole picture!

Sometimes the Scriptures are like that. Sometimes in one piece we see the whole picture. Genesis 3 is a passage in which we see a whole picture of the heart of our Father. We have redeemed lives and redeemed relationships because we have a God who seeks us when we are hiding, brings redemption when we fall, covers our lives at the cost of His own, and guards the way to the tree of life. We live with redemption and with relationships filled with life and hope because of our Father's great heart of mercy.

<h2 align="center">GROUP STUDY GUIDE
AND PERSONAL APPLICATION</h2>

1. In Genesis 1 God called each part of His creation "good." In Genesis 2, however, He proclaimed one thing in His creation "not good." What was it?

2. What need did Adam have?

3. Contrast the biblical concept of *helper* with the way our culture uses this word.

4. Genesis 2 gives us a word picture of how Eve was formed from Adam's rib. Explain why God chose a rib.

5. What must a husband do to allow his wife to know his heart?

6. Adam affirmed God's choice of Eve as his perfect complement. How can we affirm our spouses as God's perfect choice of a marriage partner?

7. After reading the text, define "leaving" and "cleaving" in your own words and tell why both are vital to a marriage relationship.

8. What does it mean to be truly naked and unashamed before your spouse?

9. As soon as Adam and Eve sinned, their relationship changed. List the physical, emotional, intellectual, and spiritual effects of sin on their marriage relationship.

10. Since the Fall, people have had a natural tendency to be emotionally closed and have great difficulty sharing their inmost selves with each other. What can we do to change this pattern?

11. As a consequence of sin, pain entered Eve's life. Describe a woman's physical and ongoing emotional pain that results from the curse.

12. The effects of Eve's sin were also seen in her relationship to Adam. Instead of being that perfect suitable helper, how did she now relate to her husband?

13. While the results of Eve's sin applied to her relationship with her husband and her children, the effects of the curse were different for Adam. What were the effects in Adam's life?

14. Man began to look to his job as his source of identity and fulfillment. List some of the problems this has caused in his home.

15. Even in the midst of the guilt of Adam and Eve's sin, what initiative did God take to minister to them?

16. Removing Adam and Eve from the Garden was part of God's judgment, but it was also an act of mercy. Explain.

REFLECTIONS

God is the One who pursues us, even when, like Adam and Eve, we hide from Him. Have you stopped running from Him and accepted Jesus' sacrifice for you at Calvary?

The effects of the curse touch each of our lives. God stands ready to comfort us when the pain we feel concerning our children becomes all consuming and we are unable to change the circumstances. Some pain, however, results from our own sinfulness. Think of ways in which you, as a woman, seek to control or "mother" your husband. Men, what are the thorns and thistles in your work, the tendency toward workaholism and losing yourself in your job? List steps you can take to overcome these effects of the curse in your life. Even with your weaknesses and failures, you can find hope in God's redemptive power.

Likewise, wives, be subject to your own husbands, so that even if some do not obey the word, they may be won without a word by the conduct of their wives—

1 Peter 3:1

3
A Sanctuary for a Husband's Heart

We looked earlier at Isaiah 55, where the prophet exhorts us to "seek the Lord while He may be found." There is no method given in the Word of God that teaches us how to seek Him. But God does promise us,

> You will seek me and find me. When you seek me with all your heart, (Jeremiah 29:13)

The heart with which we come before the Lord is always the central issue in our responses to Him. As we seek Him, He builds His heart into us and transforms our responses to one another.

We have a how-to mentality in our world today. When we begin to understand the person God desires us to be and the way He has designed us to respond to one another, we often hope that someone will give us a series of simplistic steps or a formula that will take us from where we are to where we need to be. But there are no simplistic answers for real people living in a real world in real-life relationships, and we do not find that kind of teaching in the Scriptures. Nowhere in the Bible can we find "ten steps to a successful marriage" or a formula that will result in a relationship that looks even artificially successful. God is the only "how to" in life and ministry. Only His Spirit, the words He speaks, and becoming the person He is making us to be in His Son, can enable us to live with one another the way He teaches.

When the heart of God fills our relationships, the way we respond to one another becomes characterized by His attitudes. God's love is most clearly seen in His giving of His Son for us, and in Christ's giving up His life in order that we might live. That reflects the heart of a servant. As we discuss the role of the husband and wife in marriage, it is that heart we are seeking. Christ is our "role model" for marriage relationships. The roles of a husband and a wife are essentially the same—the role of a servant. When we come to one another with that heart, all of the ministry that God desires to fulfill in our life together will overflow in abundance.

A HEART OF SUBMISSION

Even though the Word of God is clear that the husband is the head of the wife, the major Scripture passages that deal with the marriage relationship begin with the wife rather than with the husband. Although it appears that the spirit of a wife provides an environment in which her husband can grow, it is clear that this attitude of submission does not belong exclusively to her. As the apostle Paul encourages the church at Ephesus to walk in Christ, he teaches that the body of Christ is filled with relationships of mutual submission:

> And do not get drunk with wine, for that is debauchery, but be filled with the Spirit, addressing one another in psalms and hymns and spiritual songs, singing and making melody to the

Lord with all your heart, giving thanks always and for everything to God the Father in the name of our Lord Jesus Christ, submitting to one another out of reverence for Christ. (Ephesians 5:18-21)

No one in the body of Christ is continually called upon to submit to people who never need to submit in return. All of us are called to submit to one another. The only way we can give ourselves to one another and receive from each other is in an environment of mutual submission. This attitude of "placing ourselves under" another person in order to give to him or her is the key to growth in all of our relationships, especially in marriage. Even Christ, the Son of God, lived a life of submission to His Father. He said:

I can do nothing on my own. As I hear, I judge, and my judgment is just, because I seek not my own will but the will of him who sent me. (John 5:30)

Jesus did not live one moment of His life to please Himself; rather He lived every moment to please His Father. Throughout His earthly life and ministry, He always responded to His Father's initiative. As a wife responds to God's call to be subject to her husband, she is following the example of Christ in His relationship to His Father.

Wives, submit to your own husbands, as to the Lord. For the husband is the head of the wife even as Christ is the head of the church, his body, and is himself its Savior. Now as the church submits to Christ, so also wives should submit in everything to their husbands. (Ephesians 5:22-24)

A wife is to be subject to her husband as she is subject to the Lord. In fact, her submission to her husband is an expression of her submission to God. A woman can quickly see the depth of her maturity and her spirituality by looking at her heart response to her husband because her heart toward the Lord is reflected in her responses to her husband. Her marriage relationship is a mirror of her relationship with God.

LOVE IS POURED OUT

The teaching in Paul's letter to the Christians at Ephesus centers around the church. The marriage relationship is given as a picture of Christ's relationship to the church. As Christ is the head of the church, the husband is the head of the wife. When a wife lives before her husband the way God teaches her to, she demonstrates before the world the way the church responds to Christ. There is present a sense of basic authority and direction. A wife models these attitudes in her relationship with her husband.

So often we respond to this passage of Scripture with the question "How far does this submission go? Is there ever a time when I do not have to submit?" Surely there is evidence in the Scriptures that when a worldly authority is in direct conflict with the Word of God, there is justification for disobedience. But every wife must bring to God and to her husband the attitude with which Paul begins this passage: She is *free* to be submissive in everything.

It is the law that is measured out. It always asks, "How far do I have to go? How much is enough?" But love doesn't ask these questions because love is never measured out. Love is poured out.

Submission is not a mechanical response of obedience; it is the spirit with which a woman responds to her husband. A woman can be completely honest and even strongly confrontational to her husband and still be fully submissive. The spirit that God will create within her is one of support, encouragement, and protection toward her husband.

We must remember, too, that an attitude of submission is not to be confused with remaining in an abusive relationship. A woman who is being physically or sexually abused or who is placing either herself or her children in a vulnerable situation by remaining with her husband, needs to seek help quickly. Though we cannot deal with specific situations in a book like this, a woman in these circumstances should immediately seek the counsel of her pastor, her elders, or some of the "older women" in the church. If necessary, she should consult a Christian counselor.

> But I want you to understand that the head of every man is Christ, the head of a wife is her husband, and the head of Christ is God. (1 Corinthians 11:3)

As we mentioned earlier, submission is not only a woman's responsibility. Christ is the head of every man. A man who is not submitting to the Lordship of Christ in his life has no right to ask his wife to submit to him. Of course, she still must submit to him out of her obedience to the Lord, but a rebellious husband has lost his right to call his wife to a lifestyle of submission in their marriage.

> For the love of Christ controls us, because we have concluded this: that one has died for all, therefore all have died; and he died for all, that those who live might no longer live for themselves but for him who for their sake died and was raised. (2 Corinthians 5:14-15)

When a husband follows Christ's example of headship, the submission that he seeks from his wife will be stimulated by love. As the apostle Paul teaches in this Scripture, Christ's desire is to bring us to the place where all of our goals are submitted to Him and where we no longer live for ourselves but for Him. He gave His life to bring us to this place of submission. Christ loves us into submission to Him. If a husband loves his wife with this kind of giving love, his wife will respond to that love with a heart of submission. Just as in our relationship with Christ, her response of love will be stimulated by his giving. A loving husband woos his wife to a lifestyle of submission by laying down his life for her.

CHRIST'S SUPREME EXAMPLE

In Peter's first epistle, he is writing to those who have been scattered because of the overwhelming persecutions in Jerusalem. Many of these people have lost their homes, families, businesses, and hopes in this world because of these afflictions and now live as aliens in the provinces of Asia.

Peter is writing to give them hope. He tells them that even though they have lost almost everything in this world, they still have a hope that is alive, an inheritance that is imperishable, and a life that is protected by the power of God:

> Blessed be the God and Father of our Lord Jesus Christ! According to his great mercy, he has caused us to be born again to a living hope through the resurrection of Jesus Christ from the dead, to an inheritance that is imperishable, undefiled, and unfading, kept in heaven for you, who by God's power are being guarded through faith for a salvation ready to be revealed in the last time. (1 Peter 1:3-5)

Then, beginning in chapter 2, he begins to set before his readers a series of relationships of submission, teaching them—and us—to live as "aliens," or sojourners, in the midst of this world.

> Beloved, I urge you as sojourners and exiles to abstain from the passions of the flesh, which wage war against your soul. Keep your conduct among the Gentiles honorable, so that when they speak against you as evildoers, they may see your good deeds and glorify God on the day of visitation. (1 Peter 2:11-12)

Peter talks not only about our heart attitudes but also about our responses to the authorities God has placed over us:

> Be subject for the Lord's sake to every human institution, whether it be to the emperor as supreme, or to governors as sent by him to punish those who do evil and to praise those who do good....Live as people who are free, not using your freedom as a cover-up for evil, but living as servants of God. Honor everyone. Love the brotherhood. Fear God. Honor the emperor. (1 Peter 2:13-17)

In the Father's desire that we know how to handle real-life situations, the Word of God even talks about how servants should respond to their masters:

> Servants, be subject to your masters with all respect, not only to the good and gentle but also to the unjust. (1 Peter 2:18)

What Peter is describing here is an attitude that chooses submission before the world in order that God might be glorified. Now he shows us the ultimate expression of submission—the Person of Christ.

> For to this you have been called, because Christ also suffered for you, leaving you an example, so that you might follow in his steps. He committed no sin, neither was deceit found in his mouth. When he was reviled, he did not revile in return; when he suffered, he did not threaten, but continued entrusting himself to him who judges justly. (1 Peter 2:21-23)

Jesus Christ submitted to men in the midst of the trial and the cross. He did not return the evil and the pain to his persecutors but entrusted His life to His Father in heaven. As a result of His submission and obedience, Christ bore our sins, healed our lives, and redeemed us to God.

He himself bore our sins in his body on the tree, that we might die to sin and live to righteousness. By his wounds you have been healed. For you were straying like sheep, but have now returned to the Shepherd and Overseer of your souls. (1 Peter 2:24-25)

TRUST AND SUBMISSION

Peter now calls a woman to respond with that same spirit in her relationship with her husband.

Likewise, wives, be subject to your own husbands, so that even if some do not obey the word, they may be won without a word by the conduct of their wives—when they see your respectful and pure conduct. (1 Peter 3:1-2)

As we begin 1 Peter 3, we must ask, "What is Peter referring to when he says 'likewise' a wife is to be subject to her husband?" She must follow Christ's example. He is her "role model" for her life with her husband. This is a twofold response: In the same way that Christ entrusted His life to His Father in heaven, she must entrust her life to God. In the same way that Christ submitted to His Father and also to men in the midst of the Crucifixion, she must submit to her husband.

Jesus Christ would never have had the freedom to submit to men in the trial and at the cross if He had not first entrusted His life to His Father in heaven. Likewise if a wife has not entrusted her life to God, she will have no freedom to submit to her husband.

Peter gives hope to a wife who is living with a "disobedient" husband. This man may not be a Christian, or he may be a believer living in disobedience in some area of his life. While he may be won by the behavior of his wife, it may be that he will never change. This wife could live submissively with him, doing everything God desires her to do in response to her husband, and he could still remain rebellious. How Satan would love to take all of the responsibility for this man's life and rebellion and place it on the wife, saying, "If you were submitting to your husband, he would be changing. Since he is not changing, you must not be doing it right." No! She could be completely obedient to her Father and submissive to her husband, and he may still remain unchanged. If he does not change, the responsibility for his life does not rest with his wife. He is responsible for his own heart before the Lord.

Peter describes the behavior that can transform a husband as "respectful and pure." A woman brings to her husband a spirit filled with holiness and reverence. There are no mixed motives and no manipulations in her responses.

Submission is sometimes perceived as a tool that a woman might use to gain what she desires from her husband. If she is living in a painful relationship or with a selfish man, she might think, "If I do some of the things he wants me to do, perhaps I can get him to do some of the things I want him to do." There is nothing of that attitude in the Scriptures. Manipulation always devalues another person; behavior that is reverent elevates the other person with esteem.

Peter's teaching tells us two things about this woman: (1) She has made no deal with God, and (2) she is playing no games with her husband. This woman has not tried everything she can think of to change her husband and then sees this teaching about submission and says, "Okay, God, I'll try it your way for six months, and if it doesn't work, I'll go back to the old things I was doing." No! Her husband might never change, yet this woman must still come before him with a heart of submission—because that is how her Father calls her to respond.

There is always only one reason to do what God tells us to do: He is God and He calls us to obedience. This teaching is not right because it works; it is right because it comes from God. This woman's heart is holy before God; she desires wholeheartedly to please Him. She elevates her husband with esteem rather than devaluing him with manipulative games.

God says the man may be "won over without a word." How important it is for a woman (and for a man as well) to understand that her power is not in the words she speaks but in her spirit! The man is not nagged into responding; he is not worn down; he is not convinced by his wife's arguments. It is because of her spirit that he is changed.

AN ENDURING INNER BEAUTY

Peter now shifts the focus of a woman from the external to the internal as he continues his teaching:

> Do not let your adorning be external—the braiding of hair, the wearing of gold, or the putting on of clothing—but let your adorning be the hidden person of the heart with the imperishable beauty of a gentle and quiet spirit, which in God's sight is very precious. (1 Peter 3:3-4)

A woman's true beauty is not in her outward appearance but in her inner person. God calls a woman to focus not upon her physical attractiveness—that is, the way she wears her hair, her makeup, her clothes or jewelry—but upon her inner beauty, which Peter describes as a "gentle and quiet spirit." God's value system is different from the one the world thrusts upon us. Those things that are so important to this world fade away with time. What is valuable to God grows in beauty over the years and never fades away. A woman's ability to attract her husband—and the powerful and beautiful spirit with which she responds to him—grow from deep within her.

Peter is not focusing on verbal quietness here; he is describing a gentle and quiet spirit. This woman has all the freedom she desires to share her thoughts, her feelings, her ideas, her hopes, and her dreams with her husband. It is her inner spirit that is quiet. We can visualize a man who comes home from work one day with great excitement. His boss has just told him that his work has been excellent and that he has been so productive that there could very well be some real advancements and substantial pay increases in the future. He has hardly begun to tell his wife when she reacts: "It won't happen. It *never* happens. You will fail, and your boss won't come through." Her inner spirit is reacting against her husband. But Peter is describing a woman whose spirit is free to be quiet in the presence of her husband.

Some Bible versions translate this phrase as a "meek and quiet" spirit. Because of our cultural images, we have great difficulty understanding this truth. To us, meekness is equated with weakness and passivity, so we immediately picture a woman who is used, walked upon, and devalued, who passively receives anything that comes her way. Nothing could be further from God's truth!

Meekness has nothing to do with weakness and passivity; in fact, it has everything to do with power. People who are meek live according to the power of God. They allow His power to flow through them in all circumstances, in every situation, in all of their relationships. God referred to Moses as the meekest man who ever lived (Numbers 12:3), and yet, what a man of power and resource Moses was! Experiencing God's power in our relationships and circumstances brings freedom and deliverance. This has always been God's encouragement to His people:

> For the eyes of the LORD run to and fro throughout the whole earth, to give strong support to those whose heart is blameless toward him. (2 Chronicles 16:9)

73

We have no need for weak women in the body of Christ or in our Christian homes. We have a great need for women of power, resource, true beauty, and dignity. That is the woman Peter is describing here.

Peter now gives us the reason for this woman's gentle and quiet spirit in the presence of her husband:

> For this is how the holy women who hoped in God used to adorn themselves, by submitting to their husbands, (1 Peter 3:5)

This woman has taken all of her hopes, her dreams, and her expectation for her life and has lifted them off her husband and transferred them to God. Now she is free to respond to her husband with gentleness and quietness and to become a sanctuary for his heart.

A SANCTUARY FOR THE HEART OF HER HUSBAND

Often in our culture, from a very early age a young woman will begin to dream about the kind of man she will someday marry. Maybe he will be very much like her father or, if she has come from a pain-filled family, a man very different from her father. As she visualizes this man, she sees him as strong and sensitive, a giver. He will care for her, be a protector, and give direction to their lives, their walk with the Lord, and the ministry they will share.

She may dream about having a family. She sees her children growing strong in the love that she and her husband will share. There will be stability and security for them and preparation for a life of serving Christ and His Kingdom. She can picture the house they will live in; she may even build it in her mind. It will be strong and beautiful, a place of refuge to which her husband and children can run from this competitive and pain-filled world. Characterized by peace, the rooms will be filled with laughter as the children play. This young woman may even dream of the things they will have and the places they will go.

One day she meets the man who will fulfill all her hopes and dreams! They marry, and her heart is filled with joy and confidence as she looks to the future. Then, not too long after the marriage, she begins to realize that things are not working out exactly the way she had hoped. Her husband is finishing his education and laying the foundation for his career. His heart seems consumed with his work. Children are coming, and she is crying out for her husband's help and attention, but he can't hear her. He doesn't seem to have the time or energy to pray with her or encourage her. Most of the time she and the children attend church without him. She feels more and more alone. The beautiful house she dreamed of, the things they would have, the places they would go, the ministry they would share, are always "on hold." The story of her life has become dreams deferred. This man had been the key to her hopes and dreams, and now he seems consumed with himself and what he is doing.

Often in this kind of relationship, a wife will begin to communicate to her husband that he is not fulfilling her hopes and expectations. Sometimes this communication is verbal, sometimes very subtle. In the midst of these broken dreams and failed hopes, her husband begins to see that he is not measuring up to her expectations. But rather than let this knowledge spur him on to greater accomplishments, he begins to withdraw from his wife. If the pressure continues, he may seek fulfillment—or lose himself even more—in his work, his friends, or his hobbies. He may withdraw to the point where these become places for him to hide.

Peter is encouraging a woman to transfer her hopes from her husband to God (1 Peter 3:5). When she places all of her hopes in her husband, he may become a prisoner of her expectations. His own spirit can become squelched as he sees the hopes of his wife unfilled. But when his wife learns to place her hopes in God, she sets her husband free to become the man God has designed him to be. Rather than destroy her husband with the pressures of dreams deferred, in her spirit she now creates an environment of encouragement in which her husband can become a godly man. In this way she becomes a sanctuary for the heart of her husband.

Again the example of Christ is of supreme importance. Peter describes how Jesus, in the midst of the threats and reviling at the trial and the cross, entrusted Himself to "Him who judges justly" (2:23). When Jesus was in the garden of Gethsemane, before He faced the onslaughts of men and Satan, He prayed thus:

> ...Father, if you are willing, remove this cup from me. Nevertheless, not my will, but yours, be done. (Luke 22:42)

Christ honestly pleaded with His Father to take that cup from Him. But there was no other way. Jesus was the unblemished Lamb that must be slain for the sins of the world. In this prayer, Christ trusted His Father's discernment about His life and about how the work of the cross fit into His eternal plan. That is the heart that God desires to give a woman. She may wish and pray with all her heart that God might have another way to work in the life of her husband. Though she may have fears and be filled with questions about the present and the future, with the Lord Jesus she "entrusts herself to Him who judges justly." She believes that God is discerning correctly the needs of her life and the needs of her husband and the way in which it all fits into His eternal plan. She trusts God for the fulfillment of His will in her life and in the life of her husband.

HEALING AND REDEMPTION

When Jesus came before His Father with a heart that trusted

completely, fully submitted to His will, He became a vessel through whom God poured out His life to us and brought healing and redemption:

> He himself bore our sins in his body on the tree, that we might die to sin and live to righteousness. By his wounds you have been healed. (1 Peter 2:24)

So it will be with a godly wife. As she comes with this same kind of spirit before her Father in heaven and before the husband He has given her, she will become a vessel through whom God will pour His life into the life of her husband. This woman has learned a great lesson. She cannot change her husband. Only God can do that. But she can create a place in her spirit in which her husband can respond to her and to the Lord.

Some years ago my wife Karen and I were attending a small church in the Chicago area. A young couple had moved into town, and the wife had begun to attend our church. The husband was an unbeliever and had no interest in attending.

One day the pastor of our church called and asked if I would join him in visiting this couple. Since I enjoyed spending time with the pastor, I heartily agreed. We did not call ahead to make an appointment, however, and when we arrived, the husband was visiting with one of his college friends and was rather offended that we had intruded in his evening. The pastor and I spent our evening visiting with the wife while her husband stayed in another room with his friend from college.

This young wife was a beautiful Christian woman, but her husband felt no need for Christ. As far back as he could remember, he had been supremely successful at everything he had done academically and athletically. He had graduated from an Ivy League school with both a bachelor's and a master's degree and was now working for a large company in the Chicago area. To broaden the base for his career, he was now working on a second master's degree at the University of Chicago.

At this point, early in their marriage, the wife was desirous for some of her husband's help, attention, and encouragement. Their first two children had been born, and she was exhausted with the household work. She had already given up her own promising career to care for the children. More than anything else, she wanted her husband to become a Christian. At the same time, he was becoming more and more consumed with his work and studies and saw no need for God. As a result his wife was frustrated and lonely. Although she had heard of submission, she understood it only as the manipulative game I described earlier. For a time she did say to herself, *Perhaps if I do some of the things he wants me to do, I can get him to do some of the things I want him to do.*

As she began to understand Peter's teaching in this Scripture, she said to her husband, "How can I be the wife you need me to be?"

Immediately he responded, "Spend your Sundays with me; we will have a picnic, go to the beach, or play golf together."

That was the only day in which he was not working or studying; it was also his wife's one outlet for worship and ministry. Because she had begun teaching a Sunday school class, he thought she would say, "I can't be with you on Sundays." But because she had already counseled with some of her spiritual leaders, she responded positively. This may not be the counsel that church leaders would give in every situation, but this was God's leading in this case.

A few months later, when the husband had finished his graduate work and was offered a promotion that would mean not only a great advancement to his career but a tremendous pay increase as well, he began evaluating the opportunity. Realizing that the only basis on which he knew to make life decisions was advancement and salary—not his family's needs and priorities—he went to some of the leaders of his wife's church for counsel. Because of her spirit, her encouragement and support, and the freedom she was giving him, God used his search to bring him to salvation. Today that man has a powerful ministry in his church and his family, providing encouragement to his wife, modeling godliness and holiness for his children, and preparing them to serve the Lord. I will never forget how God redeemed his life because of the spirit of his wife.

BRINGING THE FATHER'S HEART TO HER HUSBAND

Some years ago our ministry was in a very real financial crisis. We had gone through difficult times before, but now it was almost impossible to continue. At the same time, a church that I loved and knew well lost their pastor. The leaders of the church approached me and asked if I would consider being the pastor of their church. I had received other requests to pastor churches full-time but had never seriously considered them, feeling that God had called me to a ministry of teaching throughout the church at large. Now, however, I began thinking, praying, and seeking counsel from my spiritual leaders. Was God using the financial circumstances to redirect my ministry?

I know that if my wife had come to me and said anything like, "We have given this ministry our very best; no one will ever be able to say we have given up too soon. Here is an opportunity to be involved in ministry and to have a regular income, too." If she had, then like Adam, I would have "listened to the voice of my wife." Instead, she came to me and said, "We cannot do that. We know the ministry God has given us. He has always been faithful. He has always provided what we need. He will bring us through this time. We need to keep trusting Him."

79

There is no question in my mind that whatever I am as a man or as a minister, my wife, Karen, has been God's primary tool in that process. She continually brings to me the heart of God.

Sometimes as churches teach about submission, they say that a wife should submit to her husband because she realizes that God is working in her life through her husband. We must be honest with one another and with the Word of God. That is not what God is teaching us here. The woman pictured in 1 Peter 2–3 is submitting to her husband because God is working in his life through her! Look again at the example of the Lord Jesus. Christ submitted to men in the midst of the trial and the cross because He knew He was the vessel that God had chosen to raise up, through whom He would pour out His life to men. This woman now submits to her husband with that same high calling, that same full vision. She submits to her husband because she knows that she is the chosen vessel that God has raised up through whom He will pour out His life into the life of her husband, bringing healing and redemption.

We discussed earlier the effects of the curse in the life of a man. He tends to look to his "field" for his identity and fulfillment. Though he will seek bread by the sweat of his brow, there will always be thorns and thistles. There will be battles with his personal discipline, problems with equipment, difficulties in relationships. He will come from that field with all of its thorns and thistles to the spirit of his wife, a place where he finds encouragement and strength and healing. God has created in his wife a sanctuary for his heart.

COMPLETE OBEDIENCE; COMPLETE CONFIDENCE

Peter gives Sarah as an example of the kind of woman a wife ought to be. Peter says,

...Sarah obeyed Abraham, calling him lord. And you are her children, if you do good and do not fear anything that is frightening. (1 Peter 3:6)

Sarah exhibited that gentle and quiet spirit and lived reverently before Abraham, even in frightening situations. When a woman hopes in God, she can do what He calls her to do without being frightened. The mind-set of this world says that if a woman lives submissively with her husband, he will destroy her life and devalue her as a person. She must think of herself and protect herself for the future. God's assurance here will set her free! A woman can be completely obedient and completely confident at the same time. Satan would steal away her obedience with a myriad of fears; God gives her confidence and peace. She can trust God with her life, for He is her protector.

We see God giving to all women a vision for how He will use them in the lives of their husbands. In Genesis 2 we saw the picture of a wife's ministry as a sanctuary for the heart of her husband. Peter gives us the same picture here. A godly woman can create an environment by her spirit in which her husband can grow into everything God has designed him to be.

Psalm 31 is one of my favorite Scripture passages because of David's honesty about his heart in the midst of great battles. Often he is in the depths of despair and then soars to the heights of ecstasy. David says two things of overwhelming significance to a woman who needs to trust in God. First of all, he says: "You are my God. My times are in your hand." (Psalm 31:14-15)

Any woman who can put this Scripture in her heart alongside one we studied briefly in 1 Peter 1:5 (you are shielded by God's power) can live fully the ministry God has given her for her husband. When she realizes that all of her times and the times of her children are in the hands of a sovereign God, she is free. God has a sovereign timetable for her life, for the life of her husband, and for the relationship they will share. Not only are her times in His hands; she also lives protected by His power. Not for one moment of her life, in any situation, in any relationship, is she outside the protection of her Father's power. Her heart is secure.

It is in this same psalm that David says,

> ...you have not delivered me into the hand of the enemy; you have set my feet in a broad place. (Psalm 31:8)

God sets our feet in a "spacious place"! This world pressures us to conform to all of the expectations it sets before us. Apart from God we become little people tightly squeezed into little places. God gives us room to be real people! With Him we can fail and get up and walk again. With God we can run freely in the great, expanded places He has created for us by His love and power.

When a woman brings to her husband the ministry of the Lord God, she sets his feet in a large place. She gives him room to become the man God has called him to be. With her spirit of encouragement, he grows in strength and godliness. She is a gift from the heart of God to her husband and to the church of the Lord Jesus.

GROUP STUDY GUIDE
AND PERSONAL APPLICATION

1. The Bible does not give us a list of ten easy steps to follow for success in marriage. Instead, God asks us to seek Him (Jeremiah 29:13). Explain how seeking God will lead to success in all of our relationships.

2. Of utmost importance to our marriages is the way in which the role of the husband and the role of the wife are essentially the

same. What is it?

3. Because the biblical teaching of submission begins with the wife, some people have believed that submission in marriage is exclusively her responsibility. Read Ephesians 5:18-21. What is the biblical teaching of submission?

4. Describe the ways in which Jesus responded to His Father.

5. From our text, define what submission is and what it is not.

6. In entrusting His life to His Father, Jesus is our model for submission. What happens when a wife has not entrusted herself to God?

7. How does submission differ from manipulation or game playing?

8. Describe the "inner beauty" that God so highly values.

9. Often childhood dreams of marriage do not come true. How can a woman's unfulfilled expectations negatively affect the marriage relationship?

10. Where does Peter (in 1 Peter 3:5) encourage a woman to place her hope?

11. When a woman places her hope in God, what effect does that have upon her husband?

12. As we look carefully at 1 Peter 2–3, for what reason does the woman pictured there submit to her husband?

13. How does a wife's submission bring healing and redemption to her husband's life?

14. Women do not need to be frightened to do what God calls them to do. What will God give to the woman who is obedient to Him?

REFLECTIONS

From the day we are born, our lives become a quest for having our needs met. How often have you caught yourself rehearsing in your mind what you feel are your unmet needs, especially those for which you feel your spouse is responsible? Imagine what could happen if you allow God to correctly discern what your needs are and then trust Him to meet them. Picture yourself becoming like the holy women of the past, who put their hope in God, not their husbands. Husband, imagine loving your wife the same way that Christ loves the church. Remember that a loving husband woos his wife to a lifestyle of submission by laying down his life for her.

Likewise, husbands, live with your wives in an understanding way, showing honor to the woman as the weaker vessel, since they are heirs with you of the grace of life, so that your prayers may not be hindered.

1 Peter 3:7

4

A Shield Over Her Heart

Now let's look at the ministry of headship on the part of a husband to his wife. When we discuss a wife's submission, the honest response of her heart so often is, "Why am I always the one who gives?" If we study the Scriptures accurately, we see another picture. It is the husband who is called upon to give:

> Husbands, love your wives, as Christ loved the church and gave himself up for her, (Ephesians 5:25)

It is the husband who gives! In the same way that Christ is the role model for a godly wife, He is also the role model for a spiritual man. Christ loves the church. Love from God's perspective always means the commitment to give one's life in order to meet another's needs. We were cut off from God's life, and that life was in His Son. God gave His Son to die for us; Christ gave His life that we might live. It is to that kind of giving love that God calls a husband. If love were only a feeling, God could never command it in this way. We cannot be commanded to *feel* a certain way about another person. However, since love is most fully characterized by commitment and actions, it can be commanded. A husband is commanded to give himself to his wife, as Christ gave Himself for His church.

CONTROLLING OR SERVING

We began our study of the ministry of a husband and a wife to one another by saying that the role of each partner is essentially the same: the role of a servant. We have looked at how a wife is a servant to her husband with her submissive spirit, how she creates an environment in which he can grow to maturity in Christ. The husband is the "head" of his wife; God has entrusted to him the basic authority for their life together, their family, and the ministry they share.

A husband must approach this ministry of headship the same way Christ did. As the head of the church, Christ was called to give His life for her. As the head of his wife, a husband has the privilege of laying down all of his life every day for the sake of his wife.

If Christ is the model for a husband's love and headship, that example is clear:

> A dispute also arose among them, as to which of them was to be regarded as the greatest. And he said to them, "The kings of the Gentiles exercise lordship over them, and those in authority over them are called benefactors." (Luke 22:24-25)

Jesus' disciples were living on the same level as our children, competing for the highest and best positions. Christ described the way relationships are worked out in this world and then in His kingdom.

> But not so with you. Rather, let the greatest among you become as the youngest, and the leader as one who serves. (Luke 22:26)

Christ encouraged His disciples to be willing to take the lowest place, the least significant position in the eyes of the world. The person willing to "give himself up" is a true leader.

> For who is the greater, one who reclines at table or one who serves? Is it not the one who reclines at table? But I am among you as the one who serves. (Luke 22:27)

As Jesus asked the question in this verse, everyone knew the answer. It was obvious to each one listening that the most important person is the one who reclines at the table and the least important is the one who serves. The Son of God then speaks those words of great light and power: "But I am among you as one who serves"! So it is with husbands. God calls us to be the servants of our wives.

We have so much difficulty grasping these truths because of our culture's ideas about leadership. We so quickly think of position, power, and control, and we have difficulty seeing the high value of serving the way our Father does.

WHAT DOES A LEADER LOOK LIKE?

When I think of our ideas of leadership, I remember the time I was invited to teach a family conference at a church in Florida. If you travel a bit, you know just how much fun it is to go somewhere and have no idea whom you are supposed to meet. That was my experience as I walked off the plane in Orlando. Although there was no one at the gate to meet me, I figured I would find someone in the baggage-claim area.

While I was waiting for my luggage, I made a quick phone call to my office, so when my name was paged, I did not hear clearly whom I was supposed to page or where I was supposed to go. After I had claimed my suitcase, garment bag, and the box of materials I had brought for the conference, there was still no one to meet me. I do not enjoy traveling all that much; I was already a bit tired, and I am often uncomfortable in new situations. At this point my attitude was beginning to change. I began saying to myself, *I came all the way down here to teach a conference for this church; the least they could do is have someone here to help me cart around all of these bags!*

Finally, I asked directions to a page phone. "See that escalator? Go up the escalator and down the hall, and you will see a white phone on the wall." How would I get all of these bags and boxes up the escalator? I figured that if I put the suitcase in front of me on the escalator with the clothes bag in front of that and held the box of materials under my arm on the handrail, I could get it all there in one trip. But halfway up the escalator I realized that the handrail was not going as fast as the escalator stairs. I was leaning back farther all the time, frantically visualizing what was going to happen at the top. It all happened. The suitcase and garment bag tumbled off, and I scrambled to keep my balance. My words were not edifying at that time.

After making my way to the page phone, I learned that I needed to meet the people who had come for me at the other end of the concourse. At that point, I put the bags and boxes down and said, "I'm not going to haul these all over the airport. If someone wants to steal them, they are welcome to do so!"

When at last I met the pastor and his elderly father, who had come to meet me, I couldn't believe the response. Never have I received a colder reception anywhere. During the hour's drive to the church, our visit was shallow. The pastor hardly warmed up during the first part of the conference and over lunch together next day.

Just before the last session of the conference, the pastor mentioned to me that he wanted to share something with his people. He told them how he had come early to the airport to meet me. As he was driving he was asking himself, "Who is this man that God will send to teach a family conference at my church, to teach my men to be strong men and leaders in their homes? He will be tall; he will be a strong teacher; he will have a powerful personality." (If you have met me, you know that is not who I am.)

He went on to tell how he waited for that tall, powerful person to get off the plane; that man never arrived. He even checked at the desk of the airline to see if my name was on the passenger list! Then he said to his father, "Why don't we see if we can find him in the baggage-claim area?" Then he told how they had passed me on the escalator. By that time I was shrinking down in the pew, saying to myself, *When was it that they passed me on the escalator?*

The pastor then told the congregation how disappointed he was when he first met me because I did not fit his image of a leader. Then he graciously told his people that even though God did not send what he had expected, God had sent them a leader! He confessed that he had a lot to learn about leadership.

We all have much to learn about leadership. All of the images of our world are in contrast to what God is teaching us here. A leader is a servant. When God tells a man that he is the head of his wife, He is telling us that we have the great privilege and honor of being our wife's servants!

LAYING DOWN YOUR LIFE

We see the servant's heart of the Son of God most clearly the night He shared the Last Supper with His disciples:

> Now before the Feast of the Passover, when Jesus knew that his hour had come to depart out of this world to the Father, having loved his own who were in the world, he loved them to the end. (John 13:1)

Christ entered this time of ministry in full understanding and full control of all that was taking place. His heart was full of love for those whom His Father had entrusted to Him.

> During supper, when the devil had already put it into the heart of Judas Iscariot, Simon's son, to betray him, Jesus, knowing that the Father had given all things into his hands, and that he had come from God and was going back to God, rose from supper. He laid aside his outer garments, and taking a towel, tied it around his waist. (John 13:2-4)

The fact that Jesus fully understood His identity and calling manifested itself in the lowest form of servanthood and the highest form of ministry:

> Then he poured water into a basin and began to wash the disciples' feet and to wipe them with the towel that was wrapped around him. (John 13:5)

Because of Christ's high and exalted position, the disciples could not grasp why He would stoop to wash their feet. This was usually the task of the lowest servant in the household. But Jesus knew that the heart of a servant most fully expresses what it means to be Lord and how that ministry is fulfilled in the lives of others.

> You call me Teacher and Lord, and you are right, for so I am. If I then, your Lord and Teacher, have washed your feet, you also ought to wash one another's feet. For I have given you an example, that you also should do just as I have done to you. (John 13:13-15)

If Christ as head of the church took the lowest place and gave Himself even in areas where other servants were reluctant, what does it mean for a husband to be the head of his wife? That giving must come from a servant's heart, and it is manifested in a willingness to do the lowest thing in order to meet any need his wife has.

For a husband to love his wife as Christ loved the church, he must give himself up for her. Christ literally gave His life for the church. In the case of a husband, this involves having a heart attitude that enables him to lay down his life day by day for his wife. Paul is describing a lifestyle of giving to meet another's needs. The apostle John described this same attitude of continual giving in his first letter:

> By this we know love, that he laid down his life for us, and we ought to lay down our lives for the brothers. (1 John 3:16)

It would be foolish to fill these pages with insights and applications about what it means for you to give yourself up for your wife. To fulfill this ministry, we as men need to do two things: First, we need to spend time with God. We need to come to our Father in heaven with listening, sensitive, responsive hearts and ask Him to open our eyes to see our wives the way He sees them, to cause our hearts to be sensitive to their needs, to create in us the willingness to give ourselves up for them. Second, we need to spend time with our wives, really listening to them, hearing their hearts.

Perhaps what your wife needs is for you to take some time away from work to be with her for lunch or for a weekend. Maybe she needs a word of encouragement or time with you in prayer. It could be that she needs you to clean the bathroom or care for the children while she has an evening to do whatever she desires. All of these will in some ways be unique to your own relationship.

HEROES AND DREAMS

I saw a wonderful example of this a few years ago when I was invited to teach a family conference at one of the translation centers for Wycliffe Bible Translators in South America. I was

93

staying in the home of a young couple. The husband, a pilot, had come to South America about ten years earlier. His job was to fly translators to the various jungle villages where they worked on translating the Scriptures. During the couple's first two field terms, the man's wife struggled greatly to learn to adjust and cope with the challenges of living in the field. The thing she never seemed able to come to peace about was the unpredictability of her husband's flying and his frequent absences, mixed with some fear for his safety.

As her husband prayed about the effects this was having on his wife's life, he asked the Lord to help her learn to adjust or he would take it as God's leading to give up flying and serve Him in some other way. In the end he gave up flying so completely that he decided not to maintain his pilot's license. His wife had a need, and he took great joy in giving himself up for her in this way.

We can only imagine how much this brother loved to fly. He had trained for this ministry for many years, but his dreams were nothing compared to his love for his wife.

Men, you cannot find direction like that in a book. You will find it only in the heart of your Father in heaven and in the heart of your wife!

My father-in-law is a wonderful example of this to me. He is a quiet man—and a servant. I have watched him give himself up for his wife for many years, and I have seen the woman she has become, a woman of great strength, beauty, and dignity and a great resource for the church of the Lord Jesus.

That man is a hero in my eyes. Someday we will realize—perhaps not before we are with the Lord—that the real heroes in this world were not the ones who could hit a baseball over a fence or run a football past a goal line, or kick a soccer ball through a line of defenders. The real heroes among us are the men who love the women that God has given them with all of their hearts, with all of their lives. In laying down his life, a husband becomes a shield for the heart of his wife.

SETTING YOUR WIFE ASIDE FOR GOD

...that he might sanctify her, having cleansed her by the washing of water with the word, (Ephesians 5:26)

As Paul continues writing about the parallels between Christ's love for His church and the love of a husband for his wife, he describes a "setting aside to holiness" that grows out of a washing with the Word. Other Scripture passages call this sanctification, and it is a twofold process. We have records in the Old Testament of the priests sanctifying vessels that were to be used in the sacrifices. First the priests washed them clean; then they set those vessels aside to be used only for their intended purpose. (Exodus 40:4-16)

Cleansing takes place on two levels: First, in our words in conversation with one another and second, in the Word of God in preparation for setting our wives aside for the Lord. We see here a need for a husband to continually apply the Word of God to the life of his wife and to their relationship together. An important aspect of a husband's ministry will be to cleanse their life together on a day-to-day basis by means of the Scriptures. When they need direction, when they deal with failure, sin and hurt, when a rebuke is needed, or when seeking wisdom, the husband is to bring the healing, cleansing water of the Word. It is the husband's responsibility to take the lead when reconciliation is needed in the relationship. To fulfill this ministry, a husband must gain a usable knowledge of the Scriptures and know that he also needs his wife's exhortation from the Scriptures.

God is calling a husband to participate with Him in the sanctification process in the life of his wife. This is the ministry of setting his wife aside—of sanctifying her—to become everything God desires her to be. In order to do this, a husband needs to learn to see his wife through God's eyes. What are her strengths? her weaknesses? her gifts? the desires of her heart? How can she be used in ministry? She will need encouragement and prayer. Perhaps she will need practical help. If she has a ministry of teaching, will her husband be willing to stay home with the children in the evening in order for her to fulfill that ministry? Will he help her study the Scriptures in preparation? These are costly ministries, but then, we must know that giving up our selves for our wives will cost us our lives.

GROWING IN BEAUTY

...so that [Christ] might present the church to himself in splendor, without spot or wrinkle or any such thing, that she might be holy and without blemish. (Ephesians 5:27)

Christ cleansed and sanctified the church so that He might present her to Himself, glorious, pure, perfect, beautiful. She gets that way as a result of His giving love. The church is everything God desires her to be because of Christ's love for her. In the same way, a husband beautifies his wife by the way he loves her. As he gives himself to her, serves her, encourages her and affirms her, she grows in beauty and grace. He presents her to himself the way he desires her to be as a result of his giving love. Every man must look at his wife after a period of years and know that he has contributed to the woman she is becoming. If she is growing in beauty, it is because of his giving love; if she fails to measure up to his hopes, it is because he has failed to give himself for her.

There is another application that we must not miss. Christ beautified the church by His giving love in order to present her to Himself glorious, pure, and complete. As a wife grows in beauty, wholeness, purity, and godliness because of her husband's sacrificial love, it is not only so that her husband can present his wife to himself the way he desires her to be. No, a husband's ministry is far more significant than that: He must also present his wife to the Lord. As they stand before Him together, the husband will be able to say, "This is the woman my wife has become as a result of my love for her." For those of us who are married, this is perhaps our most significant stewardship in all of the days that God entrusts to us in our marriages.

VALUE AND ESTEEM

In the same way husbands should love their wives as their own bodies. He who loves his wife loves himself. For no one ever hated his own flesh, but nourishes and cherishes it, just as Christ does the church, because we are members of his body. (Ephesians 5:28-30)

As Paul is writing under the inspiration of the Holy Spirit, he seems to sense our growing frustration and feelings of inadequacy. First of all, the statement that a husband is to love his wife "as Christ loved the church" is enough to overwhelm every one of us! This is just one more reminder that the Christian life is not just difficult; it is impossible! Not one of us within ourselves can measure up to this call. Only through the resources of the living Christ (Colossians 1:27) can we be what God has called us to be.

But in another sense, many of us find this teaching to be somewhat mystical and mysterious. Our hearts want to cry out, "What does this mean? How do I do it?" Let me paraphrase what Paul tells us: "If you haven't caught on yet, think of it this way: You love your wife like you love your body." We love our bodies in two ways: by being sensitive to their needs and by responding quickly to meet those needs.

When our bodies send us hunger signals, do we say, "Okay, I'm aware of that need. If I can get to it in the next couple of weeks, I will try to take care of it"? Of course not! We are very sensitive to the needs of our bodies, and we respond quickly to meet them. That is precisely how God wants us to love our wives. We live with hearts that are sensitive to their needs, and we respond quickly with all of our resources to meet those needs.

As we fulfill this ministry, we build into our wives a sense of value and esteem. We give ourselves to them and hold them close. They are unique and precious to us and are worthy of all of our lives. Christ cares for us that way because He has called us to belong to Him.

Our wives will learn to see themselves the way we see them. If we do not have time for them, if we do not care enough to meet their needs, if we spend our lives on other priorities, our wives will realize that we don't see them as valuable, as worthy of our giving our lives to them. They will learn to view themselves in that way. But if they see that we are willing to sacrifice anything to meet their needs because we see them as worthy of everything that we are and have, they will realize their great value in our eyes. As a result of our giving our love, they will grow in value and esteem in their own eyes as well. What a wonderful gift this is to give to a wife—to nurture in her a sense of beauty, value, and esteem!

This is one of the most exalted and precious expressions of a husband's ministry to his wife. As we cherish and care for our wives, we are encouraging them to see themselves as God sees them. When we lay down our lives for our wives and give ourselves up for them, we are telling them again and again that they are precious to us and are worthy of all that we are and have. We have been given the stewardship of reflecting our Father's view of our wives back to them in the way we love them. As we faithfully serve them over the years, our wives will grow in beauty in their own eyes. What a wonderful gift to give to the woman God has entrusted to us!

> "Therefore a man shall leave his father and mother and hold fast to his wife, and the two shall become one flesh." (Ephesians 5:31)

In this verse, Paul is quoting from Genesis 2, which gives God's summary statement on the marriage relationship. For this purpose—to give all of his life for the one God has given to him—a man leaves his father and mother, cleaves to his wife, and becomes one flesh with her.

> This mystery is profound, and I am saying that it refers to Christ and the church. (Ephesians 5:32)

Although we do not fully understand how the marriage relationship can be a picture of Christ's relationship with His church, God is pleased to use this human union that has been touched by something of eternity as a mirror of the faithfulness of His eternal love.

REDEMPTION FROM THE EFFECTS OF THE CURSE

> However, let each one of you love his wife as himself, and let the wife see that she respects her husband. (Ephesians 5:33)

As the apostle Paul closes this great passage, he reminds us of two great needs in the life of a wife and in the life of a husband: First, a wife needs a husband who loves her, who gives himself to meet her needs. When we discussed the effects of the curse in the life of a woman, we saw her tendency to build her life around her children and her husband, and even to desire to control him. God uses a husband who loves his wife with God's giving love as part of the redemption process from the effects of the curse. When a woman has a husband whose first thought and primary desire is to give himself up for her, she does not need to manipulate him to get him to please her. When her husband is sensitive to her and applies the Scriptures to her daily needs, encourages her and counsels her in relationship to her children, he can help her through that process of identifying with their pain.

Second, a man needs a wife who respects him. When he goes out to that field of work, seeking fruitfulness and fulfillment, he needs her encouragement when he meets with failures, the thorns and thistles. If she reinforces his weakness and failure, if she does not believe in his abilities and in him as a person, he will be destroyed. However, if a husband knows that his wife believes in him, together they can conquer worlds! It will not matter so much what other people think of him, if he has the respect of his wife. In the heart of a wife, God brings redemption from the effects of the curse.

POWER IN PRAYER

After the apostle Peter taught on Christ as an example for wives, he applied Jesus' model to husbands:

> Likewise, husbands, live with your wives in an understanding way, showing honor to the woman as the weaker vessel, since they are heirs with you of the grace of life, so that your prayers may not be hindered. (1 Peter 3:7)

Peter is still building on the example of the Lord Jesus. Just as Christ entrusted Himself to His Father in heaven and was given the freedom to submit to men, you husbands are to follow that example in your relationship with your wives. Live with your wife with an understanding heart! A husband must know his wife—her strengths, vulnerabilities, and areas in which she is prone to struggle or failure. God says to see her as a "weaker vessel." My personal opinion is that Peter is not referring to physical or emotional weakness here but possibly to the woman's vulnerability to temptation, as Eve was beguiled by Satan.

Paul refers to this also:

> ...Adam was not deceived, but the woman was deceived and became a transgressor. (1 Timothy 2:14)

Again, God calls husbands to see their wives through His eyes. The primary exhortation is to grant her honor, to see her as fellow heirs of the gift of His life. We saw in Genesis 1 that God gave Adam and Eve a shared ministry with shared authority. He brings us back to that place in His Son. The more we see our wives the way God sees them, the more we will honor them. They will be continually elevated with esteem in our hearts and in the relationship we share.

Peter concludes this passage with the statement "so that nothing will hinder your prayers." If you have ever struggled with a weak prayer life, you may have looked for a number of causes. Perhaps you feel you lack discipline or desire. Here we see a primary cause for the weakness of our prayer lives: how we see our wives. Our attitudes toward our wives become mirrors of our relationship with God. If we desire power in our relationships with God, we will view our partners with all of the esteem and value that He gives to them.

A VISION OF LIFE SHARED

If after studying the responsibilities of husbands and wives, the focus of the husband becomes his wife's submission and the focus of the wife becomes her husband's giving of himself, their relationship will remain shallow and competitive. When the husband focuses on giving himself up for his wife and she focuses on becoming a sanctuary for her husband's heart, their relationship will be free and intimate and they will grow in oneness.

There is no insight that will change a marriage. There is only one thing that will transform our lives together, and that is having hearts of servants. Only the heart of God pouring through us to one another can give life to a relationship. If all of the competition in our marriages came from our trying to outserve one another, if all of our fights were over who got the towel and basin first to wash one another's feet—there would be nothing else we would need to learn about marriage. If God were to give us the hearts of servants toward one another, our relationships would overflow with His life and His glory.

We have seen the ministry of a wife as a vessel through whom God pours Himself into the life of her husband. Her spirit becomes an environment in which he can grow to maturity in Christ. As we have looked at the ministry of a husband, we have seen that same vision. As a husband gives himself up for his wife and lays down his life for her day by day, he becomes a vessel through whom God pours Himself into the life of his wife. What a picture of fulfilled ministry! When we live with one another as God teaches us to, we share His life fully and one another's intimately. Union and communion—with one another and with the Living God.

GROUP STUDY GUIDE
AND PERSONAL APPLICATION

1. The Scriptures exhort husbands to love their wives in the same way that Christ loves the church. From our text, define what love is. What is love not?

2. How do our cultural views affect our view of leadership?

3. Jesus' desire was to show His disciples the full extent of His

love. Explain the profound teaching Christ was giving His disciples by washing their feet.

4. How does this teaching apply to the marriage relationship?

5. In Ephesians 5, Paul teaches us about the relationship between Christ's love for His Church and a husband's love for his wife. He describes a process called sanctification. Define sanctification, and tell how a person becomes sanctified.

6. What steps can a husband take to bring about a cleansing in their daily lives together?

7. Describe how a husband helps his wife to grow in beauty and grace.

8. When Paul exhorts husbands in Ephesians 5 to love their wives in the same way that they love their own bodies, what exactly is he telling them to do?

9. How does a husband's behavior toward his wife affect her self-image?

10. Ephesians 5:33 contains exhortations for both the husband and the wife. What are they?

11. What happens when a wife reinforces her husband's weaknesses and failures?

12. By contrast, what happens when a woman respects and encourages her husband?

13. What is the key to transforming a marriage relationship?

REFLECTIONS

Our marriage relationships are reflections of our relationships with God. We talk a lot about serving God at church or in other Christian organizations, but let me challenge you to look first into your own home. Ask God to give each of you hearts that will try to outdo each other in being servants. Picture yourselves "fighting" over who gets to clean the bathroom (a modern foot-washing equivalent!).

Someday we will stand before God, and He will ask each of us about the things we did here on earth. Husband, if God were to ask you what your wife has become as a result of your love, your giving of yourself for her, what would you say? Wife, if God were to ask you what your husband has become as a result of your respect for him, your being a sanctuary for his heart, what would you say? When that day comes, may you both hear Him say, "Well done, good and faithful servants!"

Rather, speaking the truth in love, we are to grow up in every way into him who is the head, into Christ,

Ephesians 4:15

5

Loving One Another

There is only one role in God's Kingdom: the role of a servant. The roles of husbands and wives are essentially the same—to love one another and to serve one another. Our marriages should reflect not only how God relates to us but also how the members of the body of Christ relate to one another. These "one another" responsibilities, applicable to all our relationships but particularly meaningful in the marriage context, are the focus of this section.

THROUGH LOVE SERVE ONE ANOTHER

For you were called to freedom, brothers. Only do not use your freedom as an opportunity for the flesh, but through love serve one another. For the whole law is fulfilled in one word: "You shall love your neighbor as yourself." But if you bite and devour one another, watch out that you are not consumed by one another. (Galatians 5:13-15)

No relationship is more susceptible to pain and hurt than the marriage relationship. Because we know each other so well, it is much easier to hurt and even manipulate the other person in this relationship. Sometimes this is conscious; often it is subconscious. But we must always guard our marriages from innuendo and spite. Paul's exhortation to the Galatians is well taken. If we build into our relationships little hurtful statements, we take the chance of consuming one another. One sarcastic comment leads to another. Each cutting remark, even if it is offered in humor, begs for a rejoinder. Soon the conflict escalates. An innocent comment hits a raw nerve and unleashes the furor of the other person. This "nipping and biting" that characterize so many relationships may eventually destroy all that you share together.

The answer to this type of conflict is to have as our goal to serve the other person. Service flows out of love. Just as Jesus took the role of a servant in order to express His love to us, we, too, are to serve others. This is especially true in our marriages. If our goal is to serve, then we will need to evaluate each comment or action in light of that goal. How does this serve our spouses? Does it build them up? Paul writes a few verses later:

> Let us not become conceited, provoking one another, envying one another. (Galatians 5:26)

Competition destroys the fabric of a marriage. When one partner feels the need to boast or to challenge the other, then naturally the other partner will feel threatened and will feel the need to boast in return or to cut down the boastful one. The marriage relationship is simply too close to allow such infighting. Rather, we ought to see ourselves as servants and constantly consider how we can build up our partners. This is nothing unusual for Christians. We ought to do this in all of our relationships. Yet the person who is so much a servant in the church often comes home expecting to be served. Somehow we forget to carry the attitude of servanthood into our home lives and see ourselves as our partners' servants.

GIVE PREFERENCE TO ONE ANOTHER

Love one another with brotherly affection. Outdo one another in showing honor. (Romans 12:10)

The responsibilities of a servant go much deeper than actions. We must begin to truly see ourselves as each other's servants, not merely act that way. When we do, we see our partners differently; we are devoted to their well-being, including their spiritual growth. In other words, we put them first, before ourselves. We give preference to our spouses.

In marriage this is a crucial truth. When our partners are devoted to us, we cannot help but respond. When we see that they care about our well-being, we take everything they are concerned about more seriously. When others give preference to us or put us first, our natural response is to try to reciprocate. We start looking for ways to put them in the position of honor. This is the dynamic the apostle is referring to in Romans 12:10. It could be translated: "Outdo one another in showing honor."

Somehow we must lift ourselves out of the self-centeredness that causes us to expect everyone else to be our servants. Especially in marriage, we need to see ourselves as less and our partners as more.

Our goal is to give our partners the honor and recognition they deserve.

Do nothing from rivalry or conceit, but in humility count others more significant than yourselves. Let each of you look not only to his own interests, but also to the interests of others. (Philippians 2:3-4)

This is the only way to root competition out of a marriage. Rather than compete over who is most important, we should strive to see who can be the other's servant. Rather than verbally build yourself up, think through what you can say to exalt your mate. Rather than focus on what you need, focus on the other person's needs and how to meet them. Outdo one another, not in sarcasm or witty remarks, but in showing preference to one another.

BEAR ONE ANOTHER'S BURDENS

> Brothers, if anyone is caught in any transgression, you who are spiritual should restore him in a spirit of gentleness. Keep watch on yourself, lest you too be tempted. Bear one another's burdens, and so fulfill the law of Christ. For if anyone thinks he is something, when he is nothing, he deceives himself. (Galatians 6:1-3)

We carry the attitude of a servant into each area of marriage. There are times when we will have to do more than merely encourage and build up. There are times when we will see a need for restoration, for confrontation or rebuke. At these times we must come to our partners with servants' hearts. We do not point out sin in order to place ourselves above our spouses. We do so because we desire them to be all they can be. We want them to be fulfilled and to grow.

When we have the heart of a servant, we can proceed cautiously to correct our husbands or wives. Paul is careful to point out what will create in us a spirit of gentleness. First, we need to look at ourselves. Often the things that bother us the most about other people are the things of which we ourselves are most guilty. We see our faults in others more readily than we see them in ourselves. Thus, Paul wisely tells us to look to ourselves first, lest we, too, be tempted. We need to make sure our lives are straightened out in this area, otherwise we will have no authority behind our correction. Then, having dealt with the similar problems in our own lives, we can proceed to restore our partners.

Jesus teaches us the same approach in Matthew 7:

> Judge not, that you be not judged. For with the judgment you
> pronounce you will be judged, and with the measure you use it
> will be measured to you. Why do you see the speck that is in your
> brother's eye, but do not notice the log that is in your own eye?
> Or how can you say to your brother, "Let me take the speck out of
> your eye," when there is the log in your own eye? You hypocrite,
> first take the log out of your own eye, and then you will see
> clearly to take the speck out of your brother's eye. (Matthew
> 7:1-5)

We so often quote the phrase "judge not" without considering
what comes after it. Jesus tells us to first remove the problem in
our own lifes; then (verse 5) you can deal with the problems we
see in our brothers' or sisters' lives. The command not to judge
does not refer to not making a truthful assessment of problems.
It refers to our attitudes in pointing out the problems of others.
We are to go not with a spirit of condemnation but with a spirit of
restoration. We deal first with the problem in ourselves; then we
are able to deal with it compassionately and humbly in our
partners.

In marriage this is a beautiful thing. So many of the attitudes
and feelings of married couples are shared that there is rarely a
sin in our partners that we cannot first find in ourselves. Then
restoration takes place in an atmosphere of mutual confession.
We must learn to desire this upbuilding and exhortation from
our partners. Rather than be devastated by the slightest negative
comment, we should welcome their constructive criticism. The
ones who know us best and love us the most desire to see us
grow. We need to be receptive to this ministry. In many ways this
is our only hope. If our husbands or wives can't talk to us, who
can? If we can't be open to them and receive their humble correc-

tion, then to whom will we listen? Paul's exhortation to the Ephesians is so applicable to marriage:

> Rather, speaking the truth in love, we are to grow up in every way into him who is the head, into Christ, (Ephesians 4:15)

As our marriages grow in this environment of mutual ministry, we will grow into spiritual maturity.

CONFESS YOUR SINS TO ONE ANOTHER

If we are to bear one another's burdens, we must know what those burdens are. Each of us has struggles in our walk with the Lord and with one another; we all have dark corners in our lives that need enlightenment. For the most part we are all too aware of those problems. We can truly say with David, "My sin is ever before me" (Psalm 51:3). Yet God has so designed the body of Christ that we never have to be alone in bearing the weight of sin. Nowhere is this more true than in marriage:

> Therefore, confess your sins to one another and pray for one another, that you may be healed. The prayer of a righteous person has great power as it is working. (James 5:16)

God wants us to experience the freedom and cleansing of confession. All of the sins that loom so large to us and seem so ugly shrink back to manageable size when others help us deal with them. We can never hold up alone under the weight of sin, but if we are willing to confess our sins and ask for help, we will find a new source of strength. While the confession purges the soul in an emotional sense, the prayer of one's spouse is even more significant. When the person closest to you is praying with you, miracles occur, temptations are removed, guilt is dealt with. When a husband or a wife expresses acceptance of the partner in spite of sin, the relationship moves to a deeper level of commitment. There is a new closeness, a deepening of love.

BEAR WITH AND FORGIVE

Confession must be met with forgiveness. Often we are paralyzed by the unspoken question What would my mate think of me if he or she knew I do this or felt this way? The fear of rejection or condemnation keeps us from sharing deeply with our partners. We are afraid we will lose their respect, and we value their respect more than anyone else's. Therefore, we must always be ready to receive our partners' confession with an attitude of forbearance and forgiveness. This is our opportunity to extend God's love to our husbands or wives.

Often we set aside the suggestion to confess our sins to one another because we feel that our partners couldn't take it. "He wouldn't know how to handle it," or "She'd just be devastated," we say. The same can be said about any type of rebuke or criticism. Yet we are called as Christians to live out a lifestyle completely different from what we see in the world, where such comments could lead to devastation. In the body of Christ we have a different resource. We have within us a source of patience, love, and forgiveness that is foreign to the world.

God calls us to minister His love in our relationships. The marriage relationship reflects God's relationship to His people. Since God's dealings with us historically have been characterized by and centered on forbearance and forgiveness, we should expect many opportunities to demonstrate that same forbearance and forgiveness in our marriages. Marriages work not because we do not hurt each other, but because when we are hurt, we respond with love. The measure of a marriage is not the lack of problems but the ability to deal with those problems. Paul tells us how to respond in a twofold process. First, put off the old person that we were:

> But now you must put them all away: anger, wrath, malice, slander, and obscene talk from your mouth. (Colossians 3:8)

Second, put on the new person God is making us to be in Christ.

> Put on then, as God's chosen ones, holy and beloved, compassion, kindness, humility, meekness, and patience, bearing with one another and, if one has a complaint against another, forgiving each other; as the Lord has forgiven you, so you also must forgive. And above all these put on love, which binds everything together in perfect harmony. (Colossians 3:12-14)

When we are wronged, our first impulse is to react, to fight back, to lash out. Paul tells us to lay that behavior aside; rebuke it as sin; put off the old. In its place, put on compassion.

We desperately need our husbands and wives to bear with our sins. We need their support, not their anger and criticism. We need their prayers, not a lecture on how bad we are. We need our partners' forgiveness, and often we need their reassurance that God forgives us. Paul tells us the source of such forgiveness: Just as Christ forgave us, so also we should forgive. Realizing how great a debt we have been forgiven, we are free to forgive others. How great is their sin in relation to ours? God has forgiven us all our trespasses, past, present, and future. Since He has forgiven us all that debt, we should be able to show mercy on a day-to-day basis:

> Therefore let us not pass judgment on one another any longer, but rather decide never to put a stumbling block or hindrance in the way of a brother....So then let us pursue what makes for peace and for mutual upbuilding. (Romans 14:13,19)

As we bear with one another, there will be differences. Even in a marriage relationship, one person's convictions may be different from the other's. As Paul addresses the question of the weaker brother, he sets forth these two truths: (1) Do not do anything that causes your brother to violate his own conscience, and (2) Do pursue the things you have in common in order to build each other up. In other words, accept one another's differences, but do not dwell on them. In bearing with one another, we may see our partners as weaker brothers or sisters. We may feel right about a certain practice, but we will forego it out of love for our husbands or wives. Rather than focus on the weakness, sometimes the most constructive attitude is to pursue peace. Give up your rights. Honor the other person's feelings and conscience. Redirect your efforts to a mutual goal that will build both of you into what God wants you to be.

Bearing with one another, forgiving one another, and bearing one another's burdens go hand in hand. Each of these aspects of servanthood has its place in the marriage relationship. Sometimes we are called upon to confront one another about the sin we see. But we should always do so with an attitude of humility, truly seeking restoration. Sometimes we will need to confess our own sins. We should not hesitate to seek our partners' prayerful support in the areas in which we struggle. Sometimes we will be on the receiving end of their sin. At that time we have the opportunity to forgive and to assure them that God also forgives them. Then we have the joy of demonstrating God's acceptance in the most meaningful way.

ENCOURAGE ONE ANOTHER

If only our homes could be full of encouragement rather than criticism. What a contrast we could present to the world in which we are torn down by competition. Constantly seeking to get ahead, men use others to fulfill their own purposes. When we are no longer useful, we may be discarded or relegated to a menial position. Perhaps the only place we can find the strength to face the brutal competition of the world is at home. Thus, it is a sad commentary when the atmosphere in a home or a marriage relationship is full of tension and bitterness, when sarcasm flows more freely than love. Yet this is where many Christians find themselves. In our homes we need to radically refocus our thoughts. We need to see our homes and marriages as refuges from the world. We find encouragement in the book of Hebrews:

> But exhort one another every day, as long as it is called "today," that none of you may be hardened by the deceitfulness of sin. (Hebrews 3:13)

> And let us consider how to stir up one another to love and good works, (Hebrews 10:24)

The writer of Hebrews tells us that sin is deceitful. How well we know! Therefore, we constantly need to be on guard for one another, encouraging one another day by day. Perhaps nothing more quickly takes the zest out of life than discouragement—one of Satan's most effective tools. He tells us that we are failures, that we will never change, that we are imprisoned in our sins and circumstances forever. If we look around us and see little progress, we are wide open to discouragement. We start to believe what Satan tells us. What we need at a time like that is to see God at work and for someone to show us God's perspective. We need to become convinced that God is bigger than our sin, greater than our circumstances. In a word, we need encouragement.

The Scriptures tell us to take aim at a ministry of encouragement. Particularly in our marriages, we should be aware of how our partners tend to be discouraged and how we can minister to them when they are. Often when husbands or wives fall into bad moods or into times of despondency, we tend to back off. We may think that it is better to let them cool off or to work it out themselves. Yet the Scriptures call us to a far more active ministry. We are told to think about how we can prod our partners on to love and good deeds. How often do we stop and ask, "How can I encourage my partner in loving more and acting out that love with our friends?" How can we stimulate our partners to follow through with the good deeds that they are capable of? This is the ministry of encouragement. When we catch a glimpse of our spouses' potential, when we sense in a real way the activity of God in their lives, and when we share that perspective and outlook with them, that is encouragement in its purest form. God is in control; He is involved. The question is, "How can we act out the things He has given us to do?"

BE OF THE SAME MIND

Marriage is a union, not merely a partnership. When two lives become one, there is a merger of personalities. An entirely new life is formed. In its ultimate form, marriage is a unity of heart and soul and spirit. Though this takes work, it can be achieved. Because the same Spirit dwells in both partners, there is a basis for unity that the world can never know. For the same reasons, this unity should surface in the church. While we may disagree over minute doctrinal issues or even over larger questions, ultimately we have a deep unity that transcends intellectual issues. Paul explains the basis of our unity in Ephesians 4:

> There is one body and one Spirit—just as you were called to the one hope that belongs to your call—one Lord, one faith, one baptism, one God and Father of all, who is over all and through all and in all. (Ephesians 4:4-6)

The body is unified not necessarily because we share intellectual agreement but because we share one life. We are united by a common goal, a common faith, a common Lord. So it is in marriage. We should exhibit with our marriage partners a deep unity

117

that transcends all other issues. We have become one. We share one life. We must ask God how to manifest that unity.

> Live in harmony with one another. Do not be haughty, but associate with the lowly. Never be conceited. (Romans 12:16)

> May the God of endurance and encouragement grant you to live in such harmony with one another, in accord with Christ Jesus, (Romans 15:5)

One of the struggles we face in our culture is time pressure. Often couples spend very little time in actual conversation beyond what is necessary to manage the household. We need to ask more than, "What do you want for supper tonight?" or "Did you give Billy permission to go out?" Though average couples rarely talk, it is easy to see how they fall into that trap. They are tired and ready for anything but conversation when they get home from work. Often the day has been so dull that there is not much to talk about other than what's for dinner. When a family does sit down to a meal together, it is hard enough to keep order, let alone carry on a meaningful conversation. And little if any communication takes place in front of the television.

However, if we are to be of the same mind with one another, good communication is indispensable. We need to talk through our goals and perspectives, share our hopes and discouragements, and receive help in facing tomorrow. But all that takes time, and the time has to come from somewhere. Each relationship finds time in its own way. One couple may hire a babysitter once a week and go out to lunch or breakfast to talk. Another couple may find that the time after the children go to bed and before the adults turn out the lights can be set aside as a no-interruption time. Yet another couple may see that as long as they stay around the house, there is always something else competing for their time or attention. The TV begs to be turned on, the laundry has to be folded, and so on. That couple may decide to take walks together on a regular basis. No matter what works best for you, there should be several times during the week when you check in with each other to see if you are still on the same wavelength. Although setting aside such times is extremely difficult and at first may not seem worth the effort, the experience of other couples has shown that those times together soon become the most meaningful times of the entire week—the heart of the relationship.

LOVE ONE ANOTHER

The roles of husband and wife are essentially the same—to love one another. There is no role in God's kingdom except the role of a servant. We are to constantly seek ways to express our love in serving our mates. As we have seen, this means putting them first and thinking of their needs before ours. Sometimes it may mean being free to point out sin and forgiving; at other times it may mean confessing our own sin and receiving forgiveness. No matter what, our focus should be on giving and building up rather than receiving. We seek to encourage and build up our partners, not in a phony way but in a real way. It means dealing with problems as well as encouraging the good things we see.

GROUP STUDY GUIDE
AND PERSONAL APPLICATION

1. It is so easy to make negative remarks, even when we are speaking humorously to each other. But if our goal is to be a servant, what must we ask ourselves before we speak?

2. How does competition in a marriage affect the relationship?

3. To eliminate competition between spouses, what does

Philippians 2:3-4 teach us?

4. Why is it important to know each other's burdens?

5. When a person is struggling with sin in his life, how do the prayers of his spouse help him? How does it help their marriage?

6. What kinds of fears prevent us from sharing deeply with each other?

7. Because we are sinful human beings, no matter how hard we try not to, we will sometimes hurt each other. What is the measure of a Christ-centered marriage?

8. How can we make our homes refuges from the pressures of the world?

9. Why is it so vital to encourage each other?

10. Though your tendency may be to back away when your spouse is in a bad mood, what might be a better response?

11. Though we may not always agree with our spouses intellectually, what unites a Christian marriage?

12. Why is it so important to spend time together in meaningful conversation?

REFLECTIONS

Have you ever visited a wildlife refuge? Many creatures live there, protected from hunters, chemicals, bulldozers, or whatever else would threaten their peaceful existence. People need refuges, too. Our homes, when filled with smiles and encouraging words, become refuges from an often brutal world. What difference would it make in your day-to-day communication with each other if you saw "encouraging one another" as a primary ministry? Remember, a ministry of encouragement can happen only as we set aside time to be together. If you and your marriage partner do not have specific times to be alone each week, write down a day and time that would work for both of you.

Picture your home as a refuge. Do whatever might be necessary to help it become one.

Look carefully then how you walk, not as unwise but as wise, making the best use of the time, because the days are evil.

Ephesians 5:15-16

6
Priorities

If we would have marriage and family relationships that over-flow with the life of God, we must also have priorities that reflect His heart. When we look at the life of Christ as it is revealed in the Gospels, one of the things that stands out clearly is His ability to discern the difference between what was urgent and what was important.

INITIATIVE AND RESPONSE

Jesus' life was characterized by the initiative and direction of His Father and by His own response of obedience:

> I can do nothing on my own. As I hear, I judge, and my judgment is just, because I seek not my own will but the will of him who sent me. (John 5:30)

Christ demonstrated to His disciples that He was a vessel through whom God the Father was working out His will in this world, and so Jesus did those things that were pleasing to His

Father. God spoke to His Son, gave Him direction for His life and ministry, and supplied the power and resources for its fulfillment, and Christ followed through in obedience, doing only what His Father had set before Him.

Jesus' earthly life was one of responsiveness. Nothing that His disciples heard Him say or saw Him do began with Him. God was all the initiative, the resource and the direction in Christ's life. Jesus lived to do His Father's will.

> So Jesus said to them, "When you have lifted up the Son of Man, then you will know that I am he, and that I do nothing on my own authority, but speak just as the Father taught me. And he who sent me is with me. He has not left me alone, for I always do the things that are pleasing to him." (John 8:28-29)

Jesus was surrounded by people who had expectations for His time and ministry. There were demands from the disciples, the religious leaders, and the multitudes. Because Christ had learned that only what His Father was telling Him to do was truly important out of all the urgent hopes and expectations of others, His life was completely fulfilled. One of Christ's last words on the cross, just before He released His spirit to God, were "It is finished." Although we know that Jesus is referring primarily to the work of the atonement and the substitutionary sacrifice to pay for the sins of humankind, perhaps in a fuller sense as Christ came to the end of His life on earth, He was free to say to His Father, "Everything that you gave me to do on this earth is finished. Nothing is undone." What a sense of fulfillment to be able to say that at the end of one's life!

SEEING WHAT GOD SEES

One of the greatest battles in my life is with this ability to discern the difference between what is urgent and what is important.

Sometimes I even picture myself as a shortstop on a baseball team. The entire team is out taking batting practice, and I am on the field alone trying to catch the balls they are hitting. Finally, I have to give up my commitment to field them all and just try to protect myself as the balls come at me faster than I can handle them!

For every one of us, this is a great battle. We live with the demands and expectations of others; we are surrounded by circumstances, family needs, and job situations that cry out for our attention. How do we learn the difference between what is urgent and what is important? Again, we must follow Jesus' example.

> So Jesus said to them, "Truly, truly, I say to you, the Son can do nothing of his own accord, but only what he sees the Father doing. For whatever the Father does, that the Son does likewise. For the Father loves the Son and shows him all that he himself is doing. And greater works than these will he show him, so that you may marvel." (John 5:19-20)

Jesus watched to see what His Father was doing, and that is what He did! We, too, must have our eyes opened by the Holy Spirit to see what God is doing. As we study the Scriptures, as we model lives of holiness and commitment, as we watch what God is doing, our vision will be expanded to see as God sees.

DISCERNING THE VOICE OF OUR SHEPHERD

Our lives will flow not only from our ability to see what God sees but also from our ability to hear His voice. Jesus told His disciples:

> But he who enters by the door is the shepherd of the sheep. To him the gatekeeper opens. The sheep hear his voice, and he calls his own sheep by name and leads them out. When he has brought out all his own, he goes before them, and the sheep follow him, for they know his voice. (John 10:2-4)

Naked & Unashamed

In our battle to know the difference between what is urgent and what is important, we must learn to discern the voice of our Shepherd. We have the voices of this world, the voices of our own feelings, and the voice of our enemy speaking to us continually. How do we learn to hear the voice of God?

We learn to hear God's voice by listening and responding. Through the Word of God and the teaching of the spiritual leaders God has entrusted to us, the Holy Spirit speaks to us. As we hear Him and respond in obedience, our ability to discern what He is saying grows.

Just as with Christ, God desires to be the initiative in our lives and to see us become responsive vessels through whom He will work out His will in this world. The church of Jesus Christ is the environment in which our hearts and lives are shared in this process.

When we talk about priorities, one truth must undergird all of our thoughts and prayers. God has given each of us all of the time we need to do His will. Sometimes we fall into the trap of saying, "If only there were thirty hours in a day. If only there were eight days each week, then I could do everything I need to do." No, our difficulty is not in the fact that God has given us more to do than we can handle. Our battle is in the choosing, the discerning, and the responding, because God has given to each one of us all of the time we need to do all of His will!

THE PRIORITIES OF JESUS' HEART

God sent His Son not only to bring redemption to us but also to reveal His heart to us. When Jesus began His ministry, He read this passage from Isaiah 61:

"The Spirit of the Lord is upon me, because he has anointed me to proclaim good news to the poor. He has sent me to proclaim

Naked & Unashamed

liberty to the captives and recovering of sight to the blind, to set at liberty those who are oppressed, to proclaim the year of the Lord's favor." (Luke 4:18-19)

This is Christ's declaration of purpose for His life and ministry. When we study the Old Testament and see God's commitment to the poor, the captives, the blind, and the oppressed, we know that Jesus is now modeling in a visual way the priorities of His Father. When God builds into us the priorities of His heart, we will be like Jesus in giving ourselves to people who are hurting. The very ones from whom the world walks away will take center place in our hearts.

In the Lord Jesus we also see a hunger for holiness, a desire for the glory of God to be seen and for the Kingdom of God to be established. These are the things for which Jesus poured out His life. We, too, will pour out our lives for these things and will seek to build them into our children, when God gives us the heart of His Son.

THE STEWARDSHIP OF OUR HEARTS

Moses wrote Psalm 90 to describe for us the transitory nature of our lives in contrast to the eternal nature of God.

A Prayer of Moses, the man of God. Lord, you have been our dwelling place in all generations. Before the mountains were brought forth, or ever you had formed the earth and the world, from everlasting to everlasting you are God. (Psalm 90:1-2)

What a truth! The God who created the earth and the world—the One who is eternal—desires to be our dwelling place. When the everlasting God becomes the environment in which we live, that is the time at which our lives become fruitful and secure. The more the Person of God becomes the place in which we live, the more our lives become what they are meant to be.

You return man to dust and say, "Return, O children of man!"

For a thousand years in your sight are but as yesterday when it is past, or as a watch in the night." (Psalm 90:3-4)

Just as God created man out of the dust of the ground, so we return to dust when our days are past and God calls us to Himself. These days in which we live, which sometimes seem so long, are so very brief in the light of eternity:

You sweep them away as with a flood; they are like a dream, like grass that is renewed in the morning: in the morning it flourishes and is renewed; in the evening it fades and withers. (Psalm 90:5-6)

Our time here on earth is so transitory that God compares it to the grass that sprouts so quickly in the morning, and by evening is already withering. Our lives are designed for an eternal kingdom and our bodies for a temporal realm. We must always be aware that these few moments are preparation for eternity:

The years of our life are seventy, or even by reason of strength eighty; yet their span is but toil and trouble; they are soon gone, and we fly away. Who considers the power of your anger, and your wrath according to the fear of you? So teach us to number our days that we may get a heart of wisdom. (Psalm 90:10-12)

When we understand the eternal nature of God and the life He has entrusted to us, and that we have a stewardship of seventy years (or more by His grace) in which we prepare to meet Him, what is the response of our hearts? The exhortation of Moses is clear: "Teach us to live with a sense of stewardship during the days You have entrusted to us, so that when we stand before You, we may present to You a heart that has become like Your own."

That is the goal of our lives! God is intimately involved with each of our lives through a sovereign and eternal process in time. He is taking us through experiences, circumstances, and relationships and is teaching us to respond to Him in making spiritual, eternal choices. God is building into our hearts those things that fill His heart. When our days are fulfilled and we stand before Him, our gift of stewardship will be to present to Him hearts that have become like His own by means of His grace.

GOD'S PRIORITY STRUCTURE

Although we have looked at Ephesians 5 and 6 in other areas of this study, here we will examine it again. In these chapters the apostle Paul presents an amazingly clear picture of life priorities:

> Look carefully then how you walk, not as unwise but as wise, making the best use of the time, because the days are evil.(Ephesians 5:15-16)

Paul begins this section of Scripture by exhorting the Christians at Ephesus concerning their walk during the times in which they lived. Because the days were evil, they needed to make the most of each day. We, too, are living in the midst of evil days. The pressures, temptations, and ungodliness of our society surround us. Our entire realm—physical, emotional, spiritual, intellectual, political—is in need of redemption. We cannot afford to contribute to or participate in the process of using, dying, rebelling, and dissipating that has overwhelmed our world. We must be a part of God's redemptive process, and our obedience as we walk in the midst of this world system is a part of that redemption. We must make the most of our time. We are stewards of this most unique and precious gift from the Lord.

Ephesians 5:17-21: *Our Walk with God in*
The Context of the Church

Paul first deals with our own relationship with God. He exhorts us not to be foolish but to understand what the will of the

Lord is. Since we have a God of revelation and His Spirit lives within us, His will is never a mystery that we must "find out." Rather, God's will is something that we are "found in," something that He works out in our lives as we walk with Him.

Paul continues to instruct us to be filled with the Holy Spirit. In times past we may have dissipated our lives in the world, but now we become channels of the life of God to one another, to the world, and even back to Himself. Being filled with the Holy Spirit here takes place in the context of the church as together we give thanks to God, minister His Word to one another, and live out relationships of submission with each other.

Our lives must be right before God before they will be right in other areas. We desire Him above all else and come to Him to be filled by His life rather than by any other "life source" in the world. It is clear from this passage that this process can be worked out only in the context of the church. The body of Christ is an environment of relationships with the living God and with one another in which our lives can become right and we can grow into everything God desires us to be. None of us will ever have right priorities by ourselves. Not one of us is wise enough or disciplined enough to make right choices every time. We are continually in need of counsel, affirmation, encouragement, instruction, correction, and even rebuking. We need to be subject to one another in order to receive these.

Our first priority must be our relationship with God. This relationship, above all of our other priorities, can be lived out only in the environment of His church.

Ephesians 5:22-33: Our Marriage Partners

The next priority Paul discusses is our marriage partners. Of all the areas of our lives that need attention, we must always seek to give ourselves to our husbands or wives first. As we discussed in the sections on headship and submission, the ministries of husbands and wives are full of responsibilities to one another. Apart from the Person of God Himself, this is our most significant stewardship in life.

In God's lifelong process of discipleship in our lives, our marriage partners are the primary tools He uses. Likewise, we must see ourselves as primary tools that God is using to build our partners. We must be free to give to one another everything that He is making us to be and to fulfill each responsibility that is ours in loving our husbands or wives.

Fulfilling this ministry will take as many years as God gives us with our partners, and it will mean always giving the best of our hearts. Of all the demands, hopes, and expectations that face us, God desires that we always see our partners and their needs first. In His eyes that is our first responsibility.

Our ministry to our partners is higher priority than our ministry to our children. I will never forget when we brought our son, Peter, home from the hospital many years ago. Wrapped in a beautiful blanket, he weighed only a little over six pounds! Though I know that Karen had read some books about being a mother and that she had talked extensively with her own mother, nothing had prepared her for what was to come! Peter drained every ounce of her strength and every moment of her time; everything that Karen had to give, Peter was there to take. That consuming process has not let up much in the years that have followed!

Our priority is not necessarily what we spend the most time doing, otherwise sleeping or working would be number one or two for most of us. Our priority is that to which God would have us respond first. When all of the responsibilities in my life need to be fulfilled, where would God have me give the first and best of who I am? These priorities are always in tension and are always

131

moving. Sometimes something that would not normally be number one in our hearts or minds must be moved to a higher priority because of a special need or an emergency. Only as we are led by the Holy Spirit will we be able to keep all of our priorities in balance.

It takes time for us to get to know our spouses. We need to share together and experience life with a common mind-set. We need to talk, sharing our thoughts, feelings, fears, hurts and questions openly. Union and communion, the shared intimacy and sensitivity to all of life, will develop as we spend time with one another in ways that provide opportunities and stimulation for communication. Vulnerability in our relationship will grow as we make it a priority to walk through life in this way.

In order to fulfill this priority in our partners' lives, we will have to continually come to God to be taught to see our wives or husbands through His eyes. What are the needs of our partners? Where are their spiritual weaknesses? In what areas of life do they need encouragement, affirmation, confrontation, or healing? How can God use me to fulfill this ministry in the one He has entrusted to me for life? Prayer is the environment in which God will give this direction.

An obvious need in this area will be to set aside time for the fulfillment of these ministries. As we mentioned earlier, before we spend time with the children, on career responsibilities, or even on church obligations, we must spend time with our partners. At times, a partner's need will surface unexpectedly, and we will need to give up other things in order to give preference to our wives or husbands. It is at these times that our true priorities are revealed. Even at the expense of other important things, our partners remain our first and most precious responsibility.

THE PRIORITY OF COMMITMENT

We have alluded several times to the Scripture in Genesis 2 in which God calls us to have a heart of commitment to our marriage partner.

> For this reason a man will leave his father and mother and be united to his wife, and they will become one flesh. (Genesis 2:24)

Commitment in marriage is one of the highest priorities in the eyes of God, and it must be for us as well. As we see the break up of basic family structures in our society, we also see more and more people alone and in great pain. When comfort becomes our highest priority and pride motivates our most basic life decisions, relationships are consumed and lives are broken. The apostle Paul reminded the church at Corinth about commitment with these words:

> To the rest I say (I, not the Lord) that if any brother has a wife who is an unbeliever, and she consents to live with him, he should not divorce her. If any woman has a husband who is an unbeliever, and he consents to live with her, she should not divorce him. (1 Corinthians 7:12-13)

There are many hurts and failures in a Christian marriage, but when a believer is married to an unbeliever, there is even more vulnerability to pain. Because this kind of marriage will surely bring increased pressure, many in the world would want to leave a marriage in this situation. What does God say? Stay! Why? Because the presence of the believer in the marriage and family has a sanctifying effect on those in the home.

> For the unbelieving husband is made holy because of his wife, and the unbelieving wife is made holy because of her husband. Otherwise your children would be unclean, but as it is, they are holy. (1 Corinthians 7:14)

The Holy Spirit, present in a family through one believing marriage partner can "sanctify" the others there. There is a holy presence, a cleansing effect, a call to godliness on the other members of the family because of this one believing person. There can be stability and hope in this home. God uses this one act of obedience—the believing partner's willingness to remain, in spite of the real pressure, pain, and aloneness—to create an environment in which children can grow in godliness. Church history is filled with heroes who have laid down their lives for their families in this way. It is in this depth of commitment that we reflect our Father's heart and pursue His glory.

THE PRIORITY OF SEX

In Paul's teaching to the church at Corinth, he calls husbands and wives to be disciplined in their sexual relationship. He does not want the people of God to live with a "lack of self-control." We might read this and ask ourselves, *Does God want us to be careful to not have too much sex?* No. In fact, God calls us to be disciplined in order that we might share plenty of joy in our sexual relationship!

> Do not deprive one another, except perhaps by agreement for a limited time, that you may devote yourselves to prayer; but then come together again, so that Satan may not tempt you because of your lack of self-control. (1 Corinthians 7:5)

God may lead a husband and wife into a time of prayer and fasting that could even involve putting aside their sexual relationship for a time in order to seek Him. If you do that, Paul cautions us, "Come together again so that Satan will not tempt you." He is warning us not to allow long periods of time apart from one another sexually. "Do not deprive one another."

It is in our sexual thoughts and desires that Satan often

tempts us. Our sex lives can be a real battleground for spiritual warfare. This is an exciting and helpful teaching from the Word of God. A consistent and healthy sexual relationship in marriage can be a place to defeat our enemy. We can minister in a wonderful way to our partners through the joy of sexual fulfillment.

Ephesians 6:1-4: *Children*

After our relationship with God and our responsibilities to our partners, our ministry to our children is the next priority. God has entrusted to us the discipline and instruction of these precious gifts from Him.

Because the needs of children are often so demanding, what might at other times be higher priorities now needs to be set aside to meet important needs in our children. As we discussed earlier, adjusting our priorities requires flexibility, but at the same time, we must keep in focus our higher priorities of our walk with God and our lives with our partners. If we do not do this, these primary relationships will waste away during the years that the needs of our children are most demanding.

For our children, we need to set aside time for the development of relationships that will be the basis for motivating and directing them in future years. When we talk about a priority, we are talking about an order of importance for spending time and giving of our hearts and our resources. It will take time to know our children and for them to know us. If we cannot, or will not, set aside time to spend with them, playing, talking, listening, and teaching, we will not be able to fulfill the ministry of discipleship in their lives that God has entrusted to us.

As couples, we need to spend time praying for our children. In the framework of our prayer lives, we will be able to sense God's heart for the needs that our children have concerning direction, behavior, discipline, desires that need to be turned or developed.

Only as we learn to see our children through God's eyes will we be able to give to them those things that are in God's heart.

If we allow our lives to be captured by other time demands or our hearts to be owned by the desires for other things, we will never be able to give to our children the things of God. Children are the most important stewardship for any couple. One of our most significant purposes in life is preparing our children for the work of God's Kingdom. We are teaching them to give their lives for the building of His church. We must pour into them all that God is entrusting to us.

Ephesians 6:5-9: Vocation

The next priority that the apostle Paul discusses is our vocations. After our relationship with Him and our ministry to our partners and our children, God calls us to give ourselves to our vocations.

A job is a means of providing for the physical needs of our families and giving as He directs while we are serving Him in the building of His kingdom. While our labor is something God wants us to enjoy, He never sees it as something that will truly fulfill our lives. Only He can do that:

> I perceived that there is nothing better for them than to be joyful and to do good as long as they live; also that everyone should eat and drink and take pleasure in all his toil—this is God's gift to man. (Ecclesiastes 3:12-13)

For a man who is struggling with the effects of the curse—the desire to find "bread" in his field only to finds thorns and thistles—this can be a source of real conflict. Satan can use the desire, and even the illusion, of finding fulfillment in a job to cause us to give our best energy, time, and creativity to our careers rather than to our families and to God's Kingdom. Many workaholics have built great monuments of money, power, and authority in the world while their real family priorities have remained unfulfilled.

It is not only the effects of the curse we must battle; we must also confront the financial pressures of this system. How can we provide homes for our children, prepare for their education, and give them a lifestyle that is acceptable in this world? Many men have decided that these take all of their hearts and strength, and they leave the children-rearing responsibilities to their wives.

It takes time to be with our children, to share life with them, to share ourselves and God with them. Even the world's concept of quality time can be a tool of the enemy. That which is concentrated, heavy, or significant will be no substitute for just being together so we have an environment and a relationship in which we can model and share the things that make a difference in all of life. The most lasting times of teaching, the times that our children will remember many years later, will probably be those that developed spontaneously as we were walking together through life.

For us to be available to our children in this way, we will need to prioritize our time commitments. Some of us know young people who left home for marriage or to further their education and training and had a real sense of emptiness in their hearts. We may even have heard them say, "My father gave me everything I could ever want, but I never really knew my father." I have never met a young person who would not gladly give away everything his father gave him in exchange for a real knowledge of his father.

In this world of financial pressures and the desire to seek identity in a career, many women also struggle with the proper priority of a vocation. While the specific needs of any family must be worked out in an environment of prayer and counsel with the leaders of their local church, the counsel of Scripture is that the priorities of a woman should be centered around the home.

As we mentioned earlier, there are no simplistic answers provided in the Scriptures concerning our families, our ministries, and our relationships. The Scriptures make it clear that a fully developed career is surely an option for a woman (Proverbs 31:10-31) but that her heart priorities center around the home. When those priorities of her family needs are fulfilled, she is free to pursue all that God sets before her.

At the same time, however, because of the pressures of our system and the deception of our enemy, we must be prepared wisely in the battle for our families. We have great difficulty today discerning the difference between our wants and our needs, and at the same time our families are becoming weaker and weaker with every passing generation. As we referred earlier to the need to submit to one another, it would express deep wisdom on the part of a young husband and wife to go to an older couple or to an older woman and seek counsel regarding the choice of a career when there are still young children in the home:

> Older women likewise are to be reverent in behavior, not slanderers or slaves to much wine. They are to teach what is good, and so train the young women to love their husbands and children, to be self-controlled, pure, working at home, kind, and submissive to their own husbands, that the word of God may not be reviled. (Titus 2:3-5)

Ephesians 6:10-20: *Ministry*

After Paul deals with our relationship with God, our ministry to our partners and our children, the vocation He has provided to supply our needs and the needs of others, he turns to ministry in a fuller sense. He talks about spiritual warfare, about the significance of prayer in the effectiveness of the gospel, and about petitions for the saints. He is describing here our ministry within the church.

When we battle with priorities that differ from God's priorities for us, we tend to think, *I need to be better organized; I need to be more disciplined in how I spend my time.* No. The answer to our struggle with godly priorities is not better organization or more discipline or anything that comes from the flesh, because our battle with our priorities is a spiritual battle:

> For we do not wrestle against flesh and blood, but against the rulers, against the authorities, against the cosmic powers over this present darkness, against the spiritual forces of evil in the heavenly places. (Ephesians 6:12)

Prayer is the most significant aspect of the armor of God. In prayer, we do battle with God against the forces of darkness. In prayer, we participate with God in a relationship of great power in the working out of His will in the lives of our partners and our children. Prayer is the environment in which ministry takes place because the real battles of our lives and our relationships are not taking place in time and space; they are fought and won in the realm of the heavenlies.

It is not so much that ministry should come after our partners, our children, and our jobs but that ministry is the overflow when all of these other relationships are being worked out rightly with God. When our relationship with Him is filled with His Spirit and we are functioning properly within the church, when our ministry is focused on our marriage partners and the children which are our stewardship together, and when our career responsibilities are met properly, ministry overflows as God leads. Ministry is what God fulfills through us as we respond with His heart to the responsibilities He has entrusted to us.

We often tend to reduce the Scriptures that teach us about life priorities to a list of decreasing values. We see the first items on the list as most important and the last as least valuable. While with a friend from New Zealand, I was able to see clearly the word picture that Paul gives us. My friend's home town had a shopping mall with a fountain in which the water would spring up and fill a pool. The water continued to spring up as it overflowed into another pool and then another. The fountain would continue to flow until all the pools were filled.

That is the picture that God is giving us in His Word. His life flows through us until all the pools of our life responsibilities are filled. Ministry is the overflow of our lives as we walk with God.

COURSE CORRECTIONS

Our lives tend to be a series of perpetual motions in which we keep reproducing in the future the things we have done in the past. Sometimes in the midst of these perpetual motions, God will speak to us and reorient our life priorities.

When we sent the astronauts to the moon, we often heard the flight controllers tell the captain to fire one of the rockets for just a fraction of a second as a course correction so that the ship would remain on its very precise trajectory toward the moon. In the same way, God allows course corrections in our lives from time to time. They might come through the confrontation of a brother or sister, a rebuke from the Scriptures, a crisis in our relationships, or through an emotional, financial, or medical crisis.

This happened to me a few years ago. On the way home from church one Sunday afternoon during a heavy snowstorm, a car coming from the other direction lost control right in front of us, and we collided. None of our family was hurt seriously, although our sons had some minor injuries and bones around my right eye were broken. Up until that moment, I could have told you practically everything I would be doing in the next six months. But God had other plans.

I remember well two prayers that I prayed during the time I

was in the hospital. I can still see myself unpacking my shaving case in front of the bathroom mirror and praying, "God, please don't let me go home until you have fulfilled everything that You desire to do in my life in this time." In retrospect, I never would have prayed so naively again!

Actually, I did return home about ten days later, after surgery to rebuild those bones around my eye. However, that very night I began to have severe back pains. Over the next few days, the pain became so severe that I had to return to the hospital. It took a while for the doctors to diagnose the problem. Not only had I developed pneumonia in both lungs; I also had a series of pulmonary emboli (blood clots).

My physical, emotional, and spiritual health quickly began to deteriorate. After a few weeks of progress, another large clot struck on Christmas Eve. Finally, one of the doctors was honest enough to tell me that one of those clots could very well cost me my life. That was my lowest point. I was so weak physically that I could not even pull myself up in the bed or brush my own teeth. I was drained emotionally. Spiritually, I was so weak that I could hardly cry out to the Lord.

The second prayer I prayed is sealed in my memory. You might remember that Paul prayed:

> I am hard pressed between the two. My desire is to depart and be with Christ, for that is far better. But to remain in the flesh is more necessary on your account. (Philippians 1:23-24)

I turned Paul's prayer around and prayed, "I am willing to go and be with you, Lord, but I want to stay here! I want to raise my sons, to enjoy my life with my wife, to do the ministry you have entrusted to me."

What I will never forget is how everything that was so important to me before the accident, all of my work responsibilities, now became so unimportant. All of those things that could not be done without me were the farthest things from my mind. God was speaking to me about other things—about holiness and obedience, about His priorities concerning my wife and my children.

God allows these times of correction. They may come through the exhortation and cleansing of the Scriptures or through a crisis. No matter when, the time to respond to God is always when He is speaking to us.

> Therefore, as the Holy Spirit says, "Today, if you hear his voice, do not harden your hearts as in the rebellion, on the day of testing in the wilderness," (Hebrews 3:7-8)

A LIFE FULFILLED

As we return to Psalm 90 and Moses' direction for a life that prepares us for eternity, we find a prayer that expresses the real desires of our hearts. When we live the way God directs, every day becomes meaningful:

> Return, O LORD! How long? Have pity on your servants! Satisfy us in the morning with your steadfast love, that we may rejoice and be glad all our days. (Psalm 90:13-14)

Even in the difficult circumstances that God allows to enter our lives, there is continual joy:

> Make us glad for as many days as you have afflicted us, and for as many years as we have seen evil. (Psalm 90:15)

There is an inheritance of the blessings of God that lasts for generations:

> Let your work be shown to your servants, and your glorious power to their children. (Psalm 90:16)

And those things that God has done through us during our

time on this earth will have stability and permanent results:

> Let the favor of the Lord our God be upon us, and establish the work of our hands upon us; yes, establish the work of our hands! (Psalm 90:17)

When we are responsive to the Lord as He gives direction for the priorities of our lives, our hearts become like His own, filled with those things that are wise and last forever. As we stand before the Lord, we, too, will be able to say, "It is finished. The work that You have given me to do is completed." Not because we have "performed" well; in each of our lives there have been many times of weakness and failure. But one of the most beautiful things about being a Christian is that God is able to fulfill all of His will, even with weak people, who come to Him with whole hearts!

Because of His grace we will be able to say, "It is finished." Then with great joy we will hear these words from our Father:

> His master said to him, "Well done, good and faithful servant. You have been faithful over a little; I will set you over much. Enter into the joy of your master." (Matthew 25:23)

GROUP STUDY GUIDE
AND PERSONAL APPLICATION

1. Amid all the expectations that people placed on Jesus while He was on earth, what did He demonstrate was the only truly important thing for Him to do?

2. In learning to hear the voice of God, what must we do?

3. Sometimes people feel that they need more time to do all that God wants them to do. Where is the fault in their thinking?

4. Knowing that our lives are short, how then should we live?

5. Why should God's will never be a mystery to believers?

143

6. Why is the body of Christ the environment we need to help us keep right priorities?

7. How are we to view time spent with our partners as opposed to time spent with our children, on church obligations, on career responsibilities, and others?

8. First Corinthians 7:14 instructs a person with an unbelieving spouse not to leave the marriage relationship. Why?

9. Explain how a consistent and healthy sexual relationship in marriage is a way to defeat Satan.

10. The next priority in our lives after God and our spouses should be our children. For what are we to prepare our children?

11. Besides material possessions, what do children need from their fathers?

12. Where should a mother's priorities be centered?

13. Why are course corrections in our lives sometimes necessary?

REFLECTIONS

So many activities clamor for our attention. Juggling the children's school schedules, music lessons, French classes, and sports practice is only the beginning when added to our personal lists that include groceries, Bible classes, haircuts, the mall, and so much more. Yet urgent items on our schedule are not always the most important. Write out a schedule of one of your busy days of the week. Does it include time to listen to the voice of your Shepherd? Is there a specific time for your spouse? If not, consider trimming the "urgent" list and giving yourself to the things that will matter for all eternity.

Finally, all of you, have unity of mind, sympathy, brotherly love, a tender heart, and a humble mind. Do not repay evil for evil or reviling for reviling, but on the contrary, bless, for to this you were called, that you may obtain a blessing.

1 Peter 3:8-9

7
Walking in the Light

The intimacy and joy we share in Christ is the fruit of walking in the redemption God has provided for us in His Son. Even though we are redeemed, we have not become "perfect people." We are broken people living in a fallen world. We experience failure and pain because we are made of dust.

The world in which we live has taught us to respond to our hurts in marriage by hurting in return. We learn to defend ourselves from pain by returning that pain to others, especially those who are closest to us. With the lack of commitment in our culture, where we tend to run away when we experience discomfort or pressure, it is not difficult to see why our marriage relationships seem so fragile, or why even those who share the same home and bed sometimes live with invisible walls that are hardly ever taken down.

In Christ we can live naked and unashamed with one another. In Him we can share relationships that are not fragile but enduring and strong and in which the life that He gives flows deeply and freely in the openness of our love. When God's healing love is given in the midst of hurts, our relationships become a refuge for one another's lives, a refuge to which we can run for healing and affirmation.

WALKING IN THE LIGHT

The apostle John wrote his first letter to define fellowship and to invite his readers to join in deep relationship of life with God and with one another. In our world, *fellowship* does not possess a great depth of meaning. We use the word to describe a warm, comfortable, enjoyable time with our brothers and sisters. God uses this word to define an intimate communion, a depth of life freely shared that can be experienced only in Christ. After giving an invitation to this eternal level of relationships, John described the basis of fellowship:

> This is the message we have heard from him and proclaim to you, that God is light, and in him is no darkness at all. If we say we have fellowship with him while we walk in darkness, we lie and do not practice the truth. But if we walk in the light, as he is in the light, we have fellowship with one another, and the blood of Jesus his Son cleanses us from all sin. (1 John 1:5-7)

Fellowship is a result of walking in the light. In Genesis 3 we studied the responses of Adam and Eve to their sin. They immediately hid from one another, and then they hid from God. In the realm of darkness, because of their guilt and shame, they covered themselves in fear of rejection.

The darkness is a wonderful place to hide. There is a comfortableness about the darkness because everything is hidden; nothing is revealed in darkness. When all is dark around us, we can easily cover up the places where we fear being seen, known, and rejected. But there is no fellowship in the dark. In order to experience intimacy and communion, we need to walk in the light.

Christ's ministry brought Him into the realm of darkness and as a result of His healing love, restored us as His children of light. Through His Son, God transferred us from the kingdom of this world's darkness to the kingdom of light.

> He has delivered us from the domain of darkness and trans-ferred us to the kingdom of his beloved Son. (Colossians 1:13)

To walk in the light means to live exposed lives in one an-other's presence—to know the freedom to be seen as we are. In their shame, Adam and Eve covered themselves because of their fear of rejection. We can now uncover ourselves in the shared en-vironment of God's grace. Only God can give us the confidence that we will be accepted with our inadequacies, weaknesses, and failures. We are vulnerable in that kind of relationship; it is often costly. Because it does not come naturally, we must learn how to live this way. If we are not willing to walk in the light together, our relationships will remain shallow. However, if we are willing to be vulnerable, to be seen, to be known, God will give us that for which we hunger—the intimate communion that He calls fellow-ship.

The relationships we are describing in this section are a re-sult of walking in the light. As we sin against one another, hurt and fail each other, this is how God enables us to deal with the pain and to experience the intimacy, freedom, and joy that He provides in His Son.

NO FRAGILE RELATIONSHIPS

Paul wrote to the Colossians to teach us about the fullness of life that we share in Christ and about how to maintain the relation-ships of redemption He has given us.

> Put on then, as God's chosen ones, holy and beloved, compassion, kindness, humility, meekness, and patience, bearing with one another and, if one has a complaint against another, forgiving each other; as the Lord has forgiven you, so you also must forgive. And above all these put on love, which binds everything together in perfect harmony. And let the peace of Christ rule in your hearts, to which indeed you were called in one body. And be thankful. (Colossians 3:12-15)

We have our roots in God's heart of love for us, and we have been changed by His righteousness and holiness. God always brings us back to who we are in Him, and He teaches us to live out our lives and our relationships on the basis of that strong foundation. Paul tells us to put on the new person that God has made us to be in His Son—a person with a heart of compassion, characterized by kindness, humility in our relationships with God and one another, gentle in our responses, and patient with each other, just as He is with us. Paul says that with those qualities in our character, God enables us to bear with each other rather than "write each other off" when we fail. He enables us to forgive each other rather than hurt in return, to bless rather than complain continually. God's forgiveness in His Son motivates us to forgive each other, and the love that comes from Him unites our hearts and lives with an eternal bond that cannot be broken.

The fact that God calls us to bear with one another tells us that there are times when others need to bear with us! When we hurt one another by the words we speak and the things we do or what we fail to do, the reason we are able to have the deep and enduring relationships we have in Christ is not based on the fact that we will never hurt each other again. We do fail each other; we do strike out and inflict pain in our relationships when we function in the flesh. We are able to share enduring relationships because of how we respond during these times; we bear with our husbands or wives and forgive them, just as Christ has forgiven us.

The world teaches us by their words, their mind-set and their example to leave when a relationship becomes painful or when it no longer meets our expectations. This system says that we must protect our rights, that our position and identity cannot be threatened. We must leave when our relationship is no longer consistent with our personal goals or when it becomes an uncomfortable environment for growing as individuals. This message comes from Satan's foolishness and lies, and it keeps us from possessing what God has given us in Christ!

God has called us to endure with one another through times that are good or difficult, times of joy or pain, times of sickness or health, times of wealth or poverty. We have promised each other and God before witnesses that we will do that, and He gives us His love to make it possible. We cannot walk away from one another when it is no longer fun to be together; we cannot build walls to keep our partners away when it hurts to be open. God has given us the means to go through anything with one another, and as we respond with His forgiving love, we see our relationship grow stronger. There are no such things as fragile relationships in Christ—only deep, enduring, strong relationships that are cemented together by His shared love.

Remember Paul's exhortation "and be thankful"? One of the most powerful things we can do to cleanse and deepen our marriage is to thank God for one another. If we spent time in prayer, thinking of every reason we have to be thankful for our partners, it would transform our attitudes. This is a great way to do spiritual warfare against our enemy, whose lies and slander would destroy us.

Bearing Each Other's Pain

We live in a society in which our lives are filled with more pain than we can handle. Our world is competitive and threatening. In many situations, we fail to "measure up" and are continually hurt in our relationships. Even in our Christian marriages we have not learned well to be servants to each other, and we tend to carry the competitive nature of the world into our marriage relationships. By doing this, we become a part of the world's destructive process rather than a part God's process of healing and building up one another in love.

It is the nature of this life that it is filled with conflicts, pressures, and hurts. When we fail, when circumstances do not work out as we had anticipated, or when relationships are difficult, the resulting pain tends to pour out of us to our closest relationships. As a result, sometimes even our family relationships are characterized by the multiplied pain of our failures. The hurts we share and inflict may flow back and forth day after day. God teaches us and enables us to respond differently:

> Finally, all of you, have unity of mind, sympathy, brotherly love, a tender heart, and a humble mind. Do not repay evil for evil or reviling for reviling, but on the contrary, bless, for to this you were called, that you may obtain a blessing. (1 Peter 3:8-9)

Peter gives this summary statement about our relationships after teaching us about Christ's example of love and forgiveness. We have been called to follow in His steps in our suffering and in our love. Jesus bore our sins in His own body on the cross; our love for each other is demonstrated in the bearing of one another's pain.

> For to this you have been called, because Christ also suffered for you, leaving you an example, so that you might follow in his steps. He committed no sin, neither was deceit found in his

mouth. When he was reviled, he did not revile in return; when he suffered, he did not threaten, but continued entrusting himself to him who judges justly. He himself bore our sins in his body on the tree, that we might die to sin and live to righteousness. By his wounds you have been healed. (1 Peter 2:21-24)

Even though Christ was completely sinless, He was reviled by men, caused to suffer, and even put to death. However, God tells us that when Christ was reviled, He did not revile in return; when He suffered, He did not threaten in return. He responded by entrusting His life to His Father in heaven. This trust and confidence enabled Him to submit to men freely, even in the Cross, in order to fulfill His Father's will. Peter tells us that Christ bore our sins in His own body that we might live and know His healing power.

Christ is our example for loving one another. When we are insulted and hurt, when even our wives or husbands bring suffering into our lives, how do we respond? The world teaches us to hurl that pain back at them to protect ourselves from further hurts, but God calls us to bear the pain of the one He has given to us in order that we might become a part of His healing process in their lives.

REPRODUCING PAIN AND DESTROYING ONE ANOTHER

Think with me for a moment of a salesman who has not been doing well. It has been a long time since he has made a sale, and his boss has been increasing the pressure. If things do not turn around pretty quickly, he will no longer have a job. Add to that the fact that his wife has also been pressuring him. When he began this new job with all of its potential, he had bragged to her about all of the things they could have and the places they could go, but none of those things have materialized. In fact, the couple has already missed a number of house payments, and the bank

153

is about to foreclose. The salesman's wife has let him know that she will not stay with him much longer. The heart of this man is overwhelmed. He is about to lose his home, his job, and his family.

In spite of the present circumstances, however, he sees one ray of hope. There is a company in town that needs some new equipment. He has been at the factory for weeks working with plant engineers to find the best equipment for them. He has also been working with the financial experts in the office to secure that equipment at the very best price. His hopes are increasing. Because this is such a big contract, he knows that if he can get it signed, he will save his job, his home, and his family.

When the day to sign the contract arrives, he discovers that another salesman has come, used his figures and still undercut his price, and signed the contract. He can hardly even begin to handle this. His sense of himself as a man and as a provider are almost destroyed. He is filled with anger. "How can they do this to me?" he cries. He goes home, his heart consumed with pain.

His wife has not had a very good day either. She had difficulty with one of her employees and returns home to find that the children have been home alone all day—too sick to go to school but not sick enough to stay in bed. They have been playing and the house is a mess. Her in-laws have phoned to say that they are coming for a visit and will be there in time for dinner. She has nothing she can prepare quickly, and there is no time to clean the house. *What right do they have to intrude in my life like this,* she thinks angrily.

Her husband comes home and at the first cross word from his wife, all of his pain begins to spill out of him onto his wife. What does she do? She mixes it with some of her own, amplifies it, and slams it back at him! They spend the next two hours destroying each other over and over again because the pain in their lives is more than either of them can handle.

That is a normal experience in this world. We take the pain that others bring to us, amplify it, mix it with our own, reciprocate, and experience mutual destruction. Peter describes an alternative response, modeled by the Lord Jesus and empowered by His life. This world defines love in many different ways, but from God's perspective, love is a willingness to bear another person's pain with him, even for him, in order to become a source of God's healing love in return.

BUILDING UP OURSELVES; BUILDING UP ONE ANOTHER

Earlier we looked at a passage from Paul's letter to the Galatians, and I want to return to it here. Paul contrasts two responses to one another:

> For you were called to freedom, brothers. Only do not use your freedom as an opportunity for the flesh, but through love serve one another. For the whole law is fulfilled in one word: "You shall love your neighbor as yourself." (Galatians 5:13-14)

There are only two possible ways to live with one another: We will either serve ourselves through the flesh or serve one another through love.

> But if you bite and devour one another, watch out that you are not consumed by one another. (Galatians 5:15)

Paul give us an illustration no less graphic than cannibalism! In our study of Genesis 3, we saw that God made garments of skin for Adam and Eve and clothed them. They must know that because they have chosen not to draw their lives from God, other life must now continually be sacrificed in order for their lives to be maintained. They now live in this world at the expense of other life.

Naked & Unashamed

We see that same thing happening in our relationships. We either draw our lives from God and have a resource of life to give to one another, or we drain life from one another in order to build ourselves up. That is what we experience in the competitive biting that Paul is describing here. The hurtful comments, the cutting remarks, the degrading statements that destroy one another are all examples of living at the expense of another's heart and life.

The Scriptures warn us: If we bite and devour one another, we will end up consuming one another. There will be nothing left at the end of the process.

SPEAKING THE TRUTH IN LOVE

Being willing to bear the pain of the ones we love does not mean that we never let them know they are hurting us. We have a responsibility before God for their sake, as well as our own, to make them aware of their sin. The command that Paul gives concerning confronting one another about sin in our lives is applicable within marriages.

> Brothers, if anyone is caught in any transgression, you who are spiritual should restore him in a spirit of gentleness. Keep watch on yourself, lest you too be tempted. Bear one another's burdens, and so fulfill the law of Christ. (Galatians 6:1-2)

When we see husbands or wives sinning in any area, we are commanded to go and restore these brothers or sisters in a spirit of meekness. With humility, sensitivity, and compassion, not with a desire to make ourselves appear superior, we must confront the ones we love and restore them in this area.

This is our responsibility when our partners sin against us. We need to confront them about their sin. Sometimes we fail to do this because we are afraid of being hurt even more or of hurting

156

the other person; sometimes we would rather enjoy the self pity and feed on our hurt feelings than restore those whom God has brought to us. But we must confront one another in this way because we have a responsibility before God for the spiritual lives of our marriage partners.

When Paul wrote to the Ephesians about the fullness of ministry that takes place within our churches when God's Word is shared deeply, he called us to respond by holding fast to Christ and speaking the truth in love to one another. We grow in our love for another as we tell each other the truth about ourselves and the relationship we share.

> ...that we may no longer be children, tossed to and fro by the waves and carried about by every wind of doctrine, by human cunning, by craftiness in deceitful schemes. Rather, speaking the truth in love, we are to grow up in every way into him who is the head, into Christ, from whom the whole body, joined and held together by every joint with which it is equipped, when each part is working properly, makes the body grow so that it builds itself up in love. (Ephesians 4:14-16)

God has given us the freedom to be seen with our weaknesses, and the discernment to see the weaknesses in our partners. The continual cleansing and stimulation to growth that results from the freedom to tell the truth to one another is one of the most exciting and beautiful aspects of marriage. In our marriage partners, God has given us those who not only know us better than anyone else does but also share life commitments to our growth and development. We need to live together with eyes open wide to see areas in which our partners need to be confronted, and hearts sensitive to minister the love that restores. As with the disciples, we are called both to confront and to forgive. If one of these vital ministries is not practiced in our marriages, our relationships will fail to grow to maturity.

> Pay attention to yourselves! If your brother sins, rebuke him, and if he repents, forgive him, and if he sins against you seven times in the day, and turns to you seven times, saying, "I repent," you must forgive him. (Luke 17:3-4)

When we have the security and confidence that our partners love us with God's commitment love, that our partners will always accept us and are always seeking our growth as individuals, we have an environment of freedom in which our relationships can grow to maturity in Christ. We can be confronted without being threatened; we can fail and be forgiven. When we share this kind of ministry, we are stimulating one another and our lives together to grow to the fullness of Christ.

DEALING WITH ANGER QUICKLY

As Paul taught the Ephesians to speak the truth in love to one another, he also encouraged them to not let time pass before dealing with sin:

> Therefore, having put away falsehood, let each one of you speak the truth with his neighbor, for we are members one of another. Be angry and do not sin; do not let the sun go down on your anger, and give no opportunity to the devil. (Ephesians 4:25-27)

We must speak the truth to each other. Sometimes we will become angry at the action of our partners as we confront them about their sin. Sometimes we will be angry as they confront us. Anger is a response that some seek to justify with no truthful basis, but sometimes we sin by not being angry when we should be. Anger is one of God's attributes and emotions, and anyone who shares God's nature will share that emotion as well. God gives us the freedom to be angry and yet not sin. We must be angry at the things that anger God. If we are not angry at the sin and depravity in this world, the devaluing of life, the casual using and destruction of people, the injustice that surrounds us, then we ourselves are committing a great sin. Not all anger is sin. Anger is also a proper, righteous response to sin.

However, we do sin when we become angry about the wrong things, when we become angry too quickly or hold on to that anger too long, or when our anger comes out in destructive ways. But this passage offers a strong warning. We must deal with anger quickly and not allow ourselves to feed on our negative feelings toward our partners. If we hold on to our anger, we will leave a door wide open for Satan to develop it into resentment and bitterness and to destroy our relationship.

One of the most important commitments any couple can make is to deal with their anger quickly, to never end their day still angry with one another. Karen and I have that unspoken commitment to one another. I do not believe that we have ever ended a day still angry with one another, but we have come close. One time in particular, we were packing to go on vacation. Karen was working in what I thought was a very slow and inefficient way. I had graciously given her my wisdom on how the work ought to be done. It had absolutely no effect! Finally, I said, "You do it however you want. I am going to bed!" I went up to bed and stewed! One of the things I have learned about anger in my life is that I do not want to put it down, because it feels so good. I kept telling myself how right I was and how wrong Karen was. However, one of the most difficult things about anger is that it never stays as anger. It quickly turns into resentment and bitterness that begin to consume relationships. Satan picks up our attitudes and begins to slander that person in our minds and hearts.

It was long past when the "sun went down" that night before I confessed my sin and sought Karen's forgiveness, but at least it was before we ended our day with one another. We have often found that the joy of making up helps to heal life's small, and large, difficulties.

> Strive for peace with everyone, and for the holiness without which no one will see the Lord. See to it that no one fails to obtain the grace of God; that no "root of bitterness" springs up and causes trouble, and by it many become defiled; that no one is sexually immoral or unholy like Esau, who sold his birthright for a single meal. For you know that afterward, when he desired to inherit the blessing, he was rejected, for he found no chance to repent, though he sought it with tears. (Hebrews 12:14-17)

Our marriages need to be characterized by the continual freedom to forgive our partners when they sin against us and to confront them as well when they need to be made aware of sin. If we fail to share with one another in this ministry of cleansing and healing, the hurts will grow into resentments, and the resentments into bitterness. This root of bitterness will destroy not only our individual lives but our marriages as well. It will eventually defile entire families. God has called us to create with Him, in our marriages and in our families, environments in which His children grow together in freedom and confidence—freedom to forgive and be forgiven and freedom to confront with meekness. Only when we share that ministry do we grow up in all aspects into Him and become strong refuges for one another's lives.

CONFESSING OUR SIN

James exhorts us to come to the Lord in all of the circumstances of our lives:

> Is anyone among you suffering? Let him pray. Is anyone cheerful? Let him sing praise. Is anyone among you sick? Let him call for the elders of the church, and let them pray over him, anointing him with oil in the name of the Lord. And the prayer of faith will save the one who is sick, and the Lord will raise him up. And

if he has committed sins, he will be forgiven. (James 5:13-15)

God is our source of help in trouble, the fountain of our joy, our healer; it is in His mercy that we find forgiveness. There is such hope in Him. Whatever our situation, He will meet us there. James then opens a foundational truth about the healing of our lives and our relationships:

> Therefore, confess your sins to one another and pray for one another, that you may be healed. The prayer of a righteous person has great power as it is working. (James 5:16)

All of our lives and our relationships need healing on a continual basis. The healing that we so desperately need is linked to the confession of sin. A man who battles with his thought life may be reluctant to share that with his wife. Although he desires so much to be holy, ungodly temptations and images often flood his mind, and he is fearful that if he tells his wife, he may lose her respect. However, she is in a more powerful position to encourage and pray for him in this area than anyone else!

With all of her heart, a woman may want to be a warm and sensitive mother, but sometimes in her exasperation with her children, her words and actions are angry and hurtful. Her reluctance to share this with her husband is based on the fear that he will no longer hold her in esteem. But who is in a more powerful position to minister to her in this area, to pray for her and to encourage her than her husband? Confessing our sins and struggles to one another is part of God's process of healing our hearts.

What stimulates healing after emotional and verbal battles in which the words and feelings are strong and hurtful? It may be pride that keeps each of us from taking responsibility, but the pain increases with the hardness of our hearts. When by God's grace one of the partners exercises the freedom to say, "I was wrong, honey. Please forgive me," at that moment a river of God's healing love is released in our relationship with one another.

God teaches us that healing is related to the confession of sin. He then sets before us one of the most encouraging passages in the Word of God:

> Elijah was a man with a nature like ours, and he prayed fervently that it might not rain, and for three years and six months it did not rain on the earth. Then he prayed again, and heaven gave rain, and the earth bore its fruit. (James 5:17-18)

When was the last time, in the midst of a great crisis, that you compared yourself to Elijah? As you cry out to God for healing, strength, wisdom, or provision, can you imagine yourself saying, "Elijah was no different than I. He was made out of dust, too. When he prayed, You answered his prayers; I need You to answer mine, too." Not one of us would ever feel free to compare ourselves with the most powerful prophet who ever lived! But God has the freedom to say to us, "Elijah had a nature just like yours. When he prayed, his prayers were powerful. You pray. Your prayers will also be filled with power." We must see ourselves through the eyes of God!

AN ENVIRONMENT OF SECURITY

As we love one another according to God's plan and share together His life commitment to meeting needs, our love becomes a strong refuge for one another's lives. Instead of being places characterized by continual pain, our marriages become environments of security in which we and our children can grow together to maturity. This is the love to which we are called; this is the way we are equipped to give the life of God to one another.

> If I speak in the tongues of men and of angels, but have not love, I am a noisy gong or a clanging cymbal. And if I have prophetic powers, and understand all mysteries and all knowledge, and if I

have all faith, so as to remove mountains, but have not love, I am nothing. If I give away all I have, and if I deliver up my body to be burned, but have not love, I gain nothing. (1 Corinthians 13:1-3)

LOVE: *1 CORINTHIANS 13:4-8*

Love is patient.

I trust God's timing for maturity in every area of your life.

Love is kind.

I look upon you with compassion, the way God does with me.

Love does not envy.

I am not possessive of you. I do not own you, your time, or your abilities.

Love does not boast.

I will not seek to focus your attention on me or on what I have accomplished.

Love is not arrogant.

I will never flaunt anything of myself before you.

Love is not rude.

My love for you has character and pure motives.

Love does not insist on its own way.

I will never use you to gain my own selfish goals.

Love is not irritable.

I am slow to anger with you, the way God is with me.

Love is not resentful.

I will not keep an account of your sins in order to use them against you at another time.

Love does not rejoice at wrongdoing.

I do not enjoy it when you fail or when you fall into sin.

Love rejoices with the truth.

I am filled with joy when your life and the relationship we share are characterized by all that is right.

Love bears all things.

I will shelter you in my giving and in the commitment of my life to you.

Love believes all things.

I will never second-guess you or doubt your word.

Love hopes all things.

All of the love that fills eternity will be ours to share together!

Love endures all things.

There is no basis on which I would ever leave you; nothing could diminish my love for you.

Love never ends.

We may fail one another, but God's love, which binds us, will cause us always to triumph together in Him.

Love never ends. As for prophecies, they will pass away; as for tongues, they will cease; as for knowledge, it will pass away. For we know in part and we prophesy in part, but when the perfect comes, the partial will pass away. When I was a child, I spoke like a child, I thought like a child, I reasoned like a child. When I became a man, I gave up childish ways. For now we see in a mirror dimly, but then face to face. Now I know in part; then I shall know fully, even as I have been fully known. So now faith, hope, and love abide, these three; but the greatest of these is love. (1 Corinthians 13:8-13)

GROUP STUDY GUIDE
AND PERSONAL APPLICATION

1. John writes to us about the fellowship that believers have with one another (1 John 1:5-7). Give a biblical definition of fellowship.

2. How is "walking in the light" reflected in our relationships?

3. Colossians 3:1-15 lists many attributes of the believer who has been changed by Jesus' righteousness and holiness. After

reading these attributes, discuss in your group what would be the likely result if a person who has just been badly hurt by his or her spouse applied this teaching.

4. Christ's prescription for healing in family relationships is found in 1 Peter 2:21-24 and 3:8-9. What was Jesus' response to those who reviled Him?

5. Contrast the difference between drawing your life from God and draining life from each other.

6. What becomes the end result of verbally biting and devouring your spouse?

7. While some of us lash out when we are hurt, others become quiet and hold in that pain. What is our exhortation from Galatians 6:1-2 about confronting another person's sin?

8. With what attitude should we seek to restore our sinning brother or sister?

9. Why is this confrontation especially important in marriage?

10. Explain what "speaking the truth in love" means as it relates to the marriage relationship.

11. The deeper our hurt, the more difficult it is to forgive our spouse. God understands our anger, but what does He exhort us to do about it?

12. If we do not deal with our anger but instead feed on negative feelings toward another person, what is the result?

13. Why is it critical to keep a "short account" when angry with one's spouse?

14. James tells us to confess our sins to each other and pray for each other (in James 5:16). Describe the sort of healing that may take place when we obey what this verse tells us.

REFLECTIONS

Doing our own thing, walking away from hurtful relationships, demanding our own rights almost seem the norm in our present-day world. After all, everybody's doing it, so it must be okay. No, says God's Word. You are to love each other in such a way that you willingly bear that person's pain, and (even more radically) forgive him for the pain he inflicts upon you! Look again at 1 Peter 3:8-9. With what should you replace evil or insults? What will you receive when you comply? Ask God to bring this to your remembrance when you and your spouse are tempted to consume each other with hurtful words. Together you can become a part of God's healing process and enjoy a deep and enduring marriage relationship.

My son, do not despise the LORD's discipline or be weary of his reproof, for the LORD reproves him whom he loves, as a father the son in whom he delights.

Proverbs 3:11-12

8
Discipline:
Motivation to Holiness

God has entrusted to fathers and mothers the joy and responsibility of bringing the children that He gives them into relationship with their Father in heaven and teaching them to live for Him. Parents are the vehicles God uses to develop His training, or discipline, in the children of His family:

> Fathers, do not provoke your children to anger, but bring them up in the discipline and instruction of the Lord. (Ephesians 6:4)

WHAT IS DISCIPLINE?

Discipline is the channeling of God-given power, drives, energies, and resources into productive areas. God's Word contrasts two lifestyles: the dissipation that marks the children of this world and the discipline that characterizes the disciples of Jesus Christ.

> Since therefore Christ suffered in the flesh, arm yourselves with

the same way of thinking, for whoever has suffered in the flesh has ceased from sin, so as to live for the rest of the time in the flesh no longer for human passions but for the will of God. The time that is past suffices for doing what the Gentiles want to do, living in sensuality, passions, drunkenness, orgies, drinking parties, and lawless idolatry. With respect to this they are surprised when you do not join them in the same flood of debauchery, and they malign you; but they will give account to him who is ready to judge the living and the dead. (1 Peter 4:1-5)

Steam is a good illustration of both dissipation and discipline. If a pot of water is brought to a boil, the steam that rises from the water escapes and dissipates into the air. On the other hand, if steam is channeled, it can be a very powerful and productive force. We can live in these same two ways. We can take everything that God is making us to be—the resource of the life of Christ within us, the power of the Holy Spirit, the stewardship of the Word of God and our relationships in the body of Christ—and we can live as if none of those things makes any difference. We can allow all of these resources to escape into nothingness and practice a life of dissipation. Or, like steam that is channeled, we can use those God-given resources to lives that are aggressively responsive to the Lord.

A disciplined life is a channeled life. By the power of the Holy Spirit, we are channeling everything God is making us to be so that we can be fruitful persons for His glory. It is that disciplined lifestyle that we are to bring to our children.

Discipline is discipling—one person open to the Lord teaching a loved one to walk with God responsively day by day, the way Jesus lived out His relationship with His Father. Jesus was not an initiator—He was a responder, a vessel through whom God was pouring His life into the world. God was the source of that ministry and the means by which it was fulfilled. This is the way

God wants us to teach our children to live before Him:

> So Jesus said to them, "When you have lifted up the Son of Man, then you will know that I am he, and that I do nothing on my own authority, but speak just as the Father taught me. And he who sent me is with me. He has not left me alone, for I always do the things that are pleasing to him." As he was saying these things, many believed in him. (John 8:28-30)

Disciples respond out of love and obedience to God's direction and draw on the inner resources of Christ. In order to develop discipline in their children, fathers and mothers need to live disciplined lives. Since discipline, like all areas of teaching, is more caught than taught, modeling is the most powerful form of communication. When children see discipline lived out before them, they will be more likely to desire to follow the same way of life.

Often we have negative reactions to discipline because we see it as "putting a stopper" on all of our desires, drives, and energies, saying no to all the things we would really like to do. But discipline has far more to do with saying yes. Discipline is a lifestyle of saying yes to God, affirming those choices that He sets before us.

A disciplined life is a matter of priorities. The key to teaching children discipline is letting them see parents who have established the right priorities in their own lives, in their marriages, and in their families. There is a disciplined atmosphere in the home. A father who has not responded to the discipline of the Lord in his own life will never be able to effectively discipline his children and teach them to walk in the way of life that comes from God.

As we model the priorities of our Father's heart, we take every thought captive to the obedience of Christ. We hate sin and love holiness. Our prayers are consistent with those things that our Father seeks concerning the coming of His Kingdom in this world, that the earth would be filled with His glory. We give our lives for those things for which Christ gave His life; we respond to hurting people with our Father's heart of compassion. When our children see us living out this disciplined life, their hearts will be gripped to follow diligently after God.

THE ENVIRONMENT OF DISCIPLINE

Effective discipline can be exercised only within the context of a loving relationship. In marriage, discipline is shared by two people who deeply love one another; it is an act of love that draws them closer to one another and becomes a motivation to obedience. Because punishment is often given as a reaction to anger, rather than draw the two individuals involved closer to one another, it often creates fear and alienation that drive them further apart.

Discipline is never linked to condemnation; only punishment condemns. God's love gives us the freedom to discipline our children in such a way that we provide an environment in which we can lead them freely to loving obedience. Jesus' ministry to us is not one of condemnation; it is the provision of life.

> For God so loved the world, that he gave his only Son, that whoever believes in him should not perish but have eternal life. For God did not send his Son into the world to condemn the world, but in order that the world might be saved through him. (John 3:16-17)

God does not punish His children in the sense of condemning them. Christ took all of our condemnation and punishment at the cross. God does not desire a relationship that is based on our fear of impending punishment. The fear of the Lord is an awesome reverence for the Person of God, and it is that reverence that draws us to Him. The fear of this world is the trembling and shaking that fill a heart awaiting condemnation and punishment.

By this is love perfected with us, so that we may have confidence for the day of judgment, because as he is so also are we in this world. There is no fear in love, but perfect love casts out fear. For fear has to do with punishment, and whoever fears has not been perfected in love. (1 John 4:17-18)

Love motivates us to holiness and obedience—the love that God has poured out to us in His Son and our love in response to Him, empowered by the Holy Spirit, binds us to Him. We love because He first loved us. It is that love for God that we seek to stimulate within our children. Only that love will stir them to obedience and have the power to keep them holy.

We love because he first loved us. (1 John 4:19)

We need so much for God to teach us that love removes all basis for guilt, fear, and condemnation and punishment. When we sin and repent, God restores us rather than condemns us. This is the ministry of love by which parents discipline their children: always restoring and giving them direction, stability, and freedom but not condemning them for failures or wrongs.

There is therefore now no condemnation for those who are in Christ Jesus. (Romans 8:1)

As fathers delight in their children, love them, and desire the best for them, they disciplines their children into lives that are godly. It is love and discipline that solidify in children's minds that they are, in fact, children of their fathers. Because undisciplined children have never had built into them an awareness that their parents love them, questions regarding their identity and security remain in their minds.

And have you forgotten the exhortation that addresses you as sons? "My son, do not regard lightly the discipline of the Lord, nor be weary when reproved by him. For the Lord disciplines the one he loves, and chastises every son whom he receives." It is for discipline that you have to endure. God is treating you as sons. For what son is there whom his father does not discipline? (Hebrews 12:5-7)

If fathers and mothers are to have an effective ministry of discipline in the lives of their children, they must cultivate and develop a love relationship with them. This begins as soon as they bring their children into the home. If fathers do not actively love their children—play with them, be available to them, give themselves to them—they have not earned the right to discipline them. It is this deeply developed love relationship that makes all of discipline effective.

Discipline without a developed love relationship becomes punishment that develops fear, anger, and alienation. When children become too old to be "spanked" or when the power that fathers have over their children can no longer be based on the fact that they are "bigger" than their children, the degree of the love that he has developed in his children toward him will be the limit of his power to motivate them. Discipline is the motivation of love toward Christlikeness.

THE REVERSAL OF DESTRUCTION

Some of us are the products of home environments in which our parents practiced punishment rather than discipline. Instead of having parents who lovingly motivated us to do what was right, we may have had parents whose punishment produced attitudes of fear and resentment in us. Unless the hurts of these experiences are healed by God's love and mercy, the pain that has been inflicted in children's lives will be multiplied in the lives of their own children with increasing intensity as the sins of the fathers are poured out upon the children from generation to generation. God desires to destroy this pattern in our families:

You shall not make for yourself a carved image, or any likeness of anything that is in heaven above, or that is in the earth beneath, or that is in the water under the earth. You shall not bow down to them or serve them, for I the LORD your God am a jealous God, visiting the iniquity of the fathers on the children to the third and the fourth generation of those who hate me, but showing steadfast love to thousands of those who love me and keep my commandments. (Exodus 20:4-6)

Children may transfer the hatred and fear they feel toward their parents to God. However, if they can grasp the depths of God's loving-kindness and mercy toward them, they can learn to see their parents through God's eyes and show mercy toward them. As God becomes our Father, His power will be the source of this healing love. In His eternal love, He will even rebuild our image of a father within our minds and hearts.

Father of the fatherless and protector of widows is God in his holy habitation. (Psalm 68:5)

My own relationship with my father was characterized by pain, punishment, and alienation. He knew nothing of God's mercy or discipline motivated by love. Reaction and anger were the only motivations he seemed to understand as he responded to his children. Needless to say, our relationship with him was characterized by fear. Because I never really knew him, I have always felt an emptiness in my heart as a result of the vacuum that existed in the place God had designed for a relationship of love to thrive. I know, too, that I would have responded to my sons in the same way apart from the grace of God.

God has been rebuilding my view of a father. In His redemptive processes in my life, God has been opening my eyes to see Him as my Father, with all of the love, care, and compassion a father gives to a child. He has given me a father-in-law who has become a father to me in every way and a model to me and my sons. As I have seen more fully God's mercy in my life, He has given me the grace to know that no one taught my father to be the father I needed. God's enabling me to forgive him in the same way that He has so richly forgiven me in Christ has been part of His healing process that has set me free to be a father to my sons.

WHY IS DISCIPLINE NECESSARY?

> Folly is bound up in the heart of a child, but the rod of discipline drives it far from him. (Proverbs 22:15)

Apart from the discipline and direction of their parents, children would live lives of foolishness. Of course, many do just that. But without direction, children would move farther and farther away from God. Unless they are taught and disciplined into a way of righteousness, they will live a life of rebellion and dissipation.

HOW DO WE EFFECT CORRECTIVE DISCIPLINE?

As a result of Adam's fall, corrective discipline is necessary because a child's nature is basically selfish and rebellious until he is regenerated in Christ. Even in a godly, disciplined atmosphere, rebellion and foolishness will become evident.

The Scriptures speak of three types of corrective discipline: a rod, a reproof, and a rebuke. A rod is a rounded instrument, staff, or twig used for physical discipline. We need never fear that we will hurt a child emotionally with physical discipline as long as we exercise it in love, with gentleness and restraint, and in a godly manner:

> Do not withhold discipline from a child; if you strike him with a rod, he will not die. If you strike him with the rod, you will save his soul from Sheol. (Proverbs 23:13-14)

A reproof is a verbal admonition given to children, with the goal of testing their motives and actions in order to redirect their behavior:

A fool despises his father's instruction, but whoever heeds reproof is prudent. (Proverbs 15:5)

The rod and reproof give wisdom, but a child left to himself brings shame to his mother. (Proverbs 29:15)

For the commandment is a lamp and the teaching a light, and the reproofs of discipline are the way of life. (Proverbs 6:23)

To rebuke is to verbally expose the behavior and motives of a child in order that his attitudes and actions might be redirected.

A rebuke goes deeper into a man of understanding than a hundred blows into a fool. (Proverbs 17:10)

Better is open rebuke than hidden love. (Proverbs 27:5)

All of corrective discipline must be exercised in love with our desire always for the child, not out of anger or resentment with a desire for vindication. With a sincere desire for the child, God admonishes us to never make it difficult for our children to obey us.

Fathers, do not provoke your children, lest they become discouraged. (Colossians 3:21)

THE GOAL OF DISCIPLINE

When parents discipline their children, they motivate them to maturity, just as God does with His children. As God desires that our behavior express His holiness, we likewise desire that our children reveal His righteousness:

Therefore, preparing your minds for action, and being sober-minded, set your hope fully on the grace that will be brought

177

to you at the revelation of Jesus Christ. As obedient children, do not be conformed to the passions of your former ignorance, but as he who called you is holy, you also be holy in all your conduct, since it is written, "You shall be holy, for I am holy." (1 Peter 1:13-16)

But the right kind of behavior only, without the development of proper motivations and attitudes, is not just meaningless; it is destructive. This is why the motivation of love is the key to discipline. Our actions flow out of our heart motivations. Developing the right motivations and attitudes within those we are disciplining is our ultimate aim.

For no good tree bears bad fruit, nor again does a bad tree bear good fruit, for each tree is known by its own fruit. For figs are not gathered from thornbushes, nor are grapes picked from a bramble bush. The good person out of the good treasure of his heart produces good, and the evil person out of his evil treasure produces evil, for out of the abundance of the heart his mouth speaks. (Luke 6:43-45)

We desire to bring children to a place of submission to God's will and authority in their lives. If children never learn to submit to the will and authority of their parents, they will never learn to submit to the Lordship of Jesus Christ apart from the stern discipline of the Lord Himself.

...if you confess with your mouth that Jesus is Lord and believe in your heart that God raised him from the dead, you will be saved. For with the heart one believes and is justified, and with the mouth one confesses and is saved. (Romans 10:9-10)

When we teach our children to submit to the Lordship of Jesus Christ and model that submission in our own lives, we will cultivate an environment in which God will develop His motives in the hearts of our children. God will then motivate our sons and our daughters to become vessels through which He will express His power and His glory.

FINISHING THE RACE

The nature of punishment is that it is spent in a moment; the nature of discipline is that it is aimed at a lifetime. The writer to the Hebrews gives us a picture of the discipline of God in our lives that enables us to endure and to share His holiness.

The writer begins in chapter 11 with illustrations of those who endured in this world by means of their faith. They were able to see the reality of God and His Kingdom beyond the system of this world. Abraham did not allow the roots of his life to go deeply into this world because he knew the reality of God's coming Kingdom:

> By faith Abraham obeyed when he was called to go out to a place that he was to receive as an inheritance. And he went out, not knowing where he was going. By faith he went to live in the land of promise, as in a foreign land, living in tents with Isaac and Jacob, heirs with him of the same promise. For he was looking forward to the city that has foundations, whose designer and builder is God. (Hebrews 11:8-10)

Because of the reality of Christ, which God had revealed to him, Moses chose to endure hardships with the people of God rather than enjoy the kind of life he could have had in this world:

> By faith Moses, when he was grown up, refused to be called the son of Pharaoh's daughter, choosing rather to be mistreated with the people of God than to enjoy the fleeting pleasures of sin. He considered the reproach of Christ greater wealth than the treasures of Egypt, for he was looking to the reward. By faith he left Egypt, not being afraid of the anger of the king, for he endured as seeing him who is invisible.(Hebrews 11:24-27)

After many illustrations of enduring faith, God calls us to prepare for the race, for the test of endurance before us.

> Therefore, since we are surrounded by so great a cloud of witnesses, let us also lay aside every weight, and sin which clings so closely, and let us run with endurance the race that is set before us, (Hebrews 12:1)

Our ministry to our children is aimed at teaching them to live unencumbered lives, to not allow their roots to go deeply into this physical/temporal world. We teach them to put aside sin so that they will not be weighed down to the point of immobility. God wants us prepared to run freely over a long distance.

> ...looking to Jesus, the founder and perfecter of our faith, who for the joy that was set before him endured the cross, despising the shame, and is seated at the right hand of the throne of God. Consider him who endured from sinners such hostility against himself, so that you may not grow weary or fainthearted. (Hebrews 12:2-3)

Our children must learn to "look to" Jesus! He is the supreme illustration of discipline and endurance. In order for us to live lives that are disciplined and characterized by the endurance God desires, we must have a clear picture of the goal. We need to give our children a vision of who they are in Christ, the people He desires them to be, and the ministry He is developing in their lives. This will become a powerful motivation for them to fulfill what God is setting before them.

> In your struggle against sin you have not yet resisted to the point of shedding your blood. And have you forgotten the exhortation that addresses you as sons? "My son, do not regard lightly the discipline of the Lord, nor be weary when reproved by him. For the Lord disciplines the one he loves, and chastises every son whom he receives." (Hebrews 12:4-6)

God tells us that every son who comes to Him will be disciplined. We are called to remember this truth when we are going through difficult times. Our children must know, too, that this will be part of God's continuing process in their lives:

> It is for discipline that you have to endure. God is treating you as sons. For what son is there whom his father does not discipline? If you are left without discipline, in which all have participated, then you are illegitimate children and not sons. Besides this, we have had earthly fathers who disciplined us and we respected them. Shall we not much more be subject to the Father of spirits and live? For they disciplined us for a short time as it seemed best to them, but he disciplines us for our good, that we may share his holiness. (Hebrews 12:7-10)

It is discipline that enables us to endure, and endurance is one of the most significant character qualities that God desires to develop in His children. We must teach our children to maintain hearts that are responsive to the Lord so that they will be able to participate with Him in the development of endurance. It is through the discipline of God's love that He develops endurance within us. Endurance is far more important to God than style or speed when it comes to the race that He has for us and our children to run. He wants us to be able to run to the end and not fall before the finish line:

> For the moment all discipline seems painful rather than pleasant, but later it yields the peaceful fruit of righteousness to those who have been trained by it. (Hebrews 12:11)

It is painful and difficult to be disciplined, and it hurts us to discipline our children. God wants us to look at the fruit it yields—shared holiness with Him and a life characterized by His righteousness. The most prized and precious gift we can give to our children is to build into them a desire to know God and to become like Him in every way. This must be a lifetime commitment:

> Therefore lift your drooping hands and strengthen your weak knees, and make straight paths for your feet, so that what is lame may not be put out of joint but rather be healed. (Hebrews 12:12-13)

We are called, then, to minister strength to our children in this endurance contest, to run before them to clear the path and to straighten the blind curves and corners. When they stumble and are wounded, we are to minister God's healing life. Only in this way can they complete the race.

Discipline is a way of life; it involves living with all of the resources God has given to us channeled toward fulfilling His will. Discipline is the runner who runs miles and miles every day for months so that when the day of the race comes he can endure. God disciplines us so that on the day of the race we will have the strength to endure. When we discipline our children, we are strengthening them to run with endurance the race that God has set before them and to win the prize.

> Do you not know that in a race all the runners compete, but only one receives the prize? So run that you may obtain it. Every athlete exercises self-control in all things. They do it to receive a perishable wreath, but we an imperishable. So I do not run aimlessly; I do not box as one beating the air. But I discipline my body and keep it under control, lest after preaching to others I myself should be disqualified. (1 Corinthians 9:24-27)

GROUP STUDY GUIDE AND PERSONAL APPLICATION

1. In your own words, define discipline.

2. Contrast a disciplined life with one of dissipation.

3. How can we teach our children to live disciplined lives?

4. Explain the difference between discipline and punishment.

5. When does discipline become mere punishment?

6. We have learned from Proverbs 22:15 that discipline is essential for children because by nature they would grow up to live a life of foolishness, rebellion, and dissipation. Our task as parents is one of correction. List the three types of corrective discipline and tell when each should be used.

7. How must corrective discipline always be exercised?

8. It is important to teach our children more than just right behavior. What else is needed?

9. What must we teach our children about God's will and His authority in their lives?

10. How do we fix our eyes on Jesus and teach our children to do the same?

11. Explain why endurance is so important as we run our race.

REFLECTIONS

What a thrill it is to watch marathon runners compete for a gold medal! Yes, they have trained to improve their style and speed, yet in the end it is their ability to endure that propels them over the finish line. Our children (as well as ourselves) are in training for the race of life. When we discipline them, we strengthen them to run with endurance the race God has set before them. How would you discipline your children differently if your focus changed from short-term correction of their behavior to helping them develop endurance to finish the race?

And these words that I command you today shall be on your heart. You shall teach them diligently to your children, and shall talk of them when you sit in your house, and when you walk by the way, and when you lie down, and when you rise.

Deuteronomy 6:6-7

9
Instruction in Godliness

God has given parents the joy of the ministry of His life. In 1 Peter 3:7 God calls husbands and wives "heirs of the grace of life." The life we receive and share is not only the physical life of this world but also the eternal life of our Father. We have the responsibility of sharing God's life with our children and teaching them to live for Him. By giving them a way of life that comes from God, we share together as heirs of His life.

> Fathers, do not provoke your children to anger, but bring them up in the discipline and instruction of the Lord. (Ephesians 6:4)

This is a ministry of motivation—building with God's love and God's mind—not a program of provocation. Children can never be provoked to become like God; they must be encouraged and stimulated to desire godliness.

THE MINISTRY OF PARENTS

In our twentieth-century culture, we have often left the educational ministry of our children to schools, churches, and Sunday schools. Regarding the area of education, the Scriptures do not give the responsibility to schools but to the church and to families. However, it lays the greatest measure of responsibility for instructing children in the hands of those who can fulfill it most effectively—the parents in the home. This is God's plan. The family is God's primary vehicle through which children develop in righteousness. Although the church is the framework in which all of ministry takes place, it cannot fulfill what God has designed the family to fulfill. The church is a family of families stimulating one another to mutual growth in love.

In the family, God has placed a man and a woman who bear His image to give instruction and direction to their children and to provide warmth, empathy, and encouragement. This gives the relationships an environment in which children can develop in love and security and be healed from the wounds the outside world inflicts on them. The ministry of God's Word and God's life to children is primarily the responsibility of the parents:

> Only take care, and keep your soul diligently, lest you forget the things that your eyes have seen, and lest they depart from your heart all the days of your life. Make them known to your children and your children's children—how on the day that you stood before the LORD your God at Horeb, the LORD said to me, "Gather the people to me, that I may let them hear my words, so that they may learn to fear me all the days that they live on the earth, and that they may teach their children so." (Deuteronomy 4:9-10)

God has ordained that parents and grandparents set a pattern of life for their children and grandchildren to follow, and God has made children in such a way that they will respond to Him the way they respond to their natural father. God draws strong parallels between a natural father and His own ministry:

> As a father shows compassion to his children, so the LORD shows compassion to those who fear him. (Psalm 103:13)

God tells us that as parents build a family unit according to the design revealed in His Word, the children will follow through with God's way of life:

> Train up a child in the way he should go; even when he is old he will not depart from it. (Proverbs 22:6)

To "train up" means to practice with him, to do it until it becomes a part of him. "In the way he should go" has to do with the uniqueness of each individual child. We minister to each child and meet him where he is according to the way God has designed him. From birth, this is a ministry of creating a hunger to know God and His ways and to become like Him in every area of life.

This is a personal ministry of the parents and grandparents in the lives of each one of their children as they give themselves to the needs that are unique to each child and to his development in Christlikeness.

Karen and I have two sons, Peter and Joel. They are both incredible joys to us, and they are so different from each other that sometimes we wonder if they are actually from the same family! We have needed the wisdom of the Holy Spirit as we have raised them to the glory of God.

THE FOUNDATION OF TEACHING

> Hear, O Israel: The LORD our God, the LORD is one. (Deuteronomy 6:4)

These were the most common words on the lips of every Hebrew believer. A strong affirmation of God and the proclamation of who He is and what He is like were central to their hearts. In our teaching ministry to our children, this is what God desires us to communicate about Him. As we teach the Scriptures, model a heart focused on God, and relate His Word to real-life situations, we are developing a framework in which our children can see God, know Him and respond to Him.

As parents we must set our hearts on revealing God's attributes and His character. During the years that our Father entrusts our children to us, it is our desire for them to see that God is holy and thus to pursue holiness in their lives. As they see His sovereign control not only over the universe but also over every detail of their personal lives, they will become confident and secure in His protecting power. His heart of compassion toward them when they sin will move them to mercy in their own relationships. When they see His righteousness and justice, they also will hunger to see the poor and downtrodden elevated and vindicated. If they can understand something of God's desire for the lost to know Him, they will share His heart for evangelism and missions.

> You shall love the LORD your God with all your heart and with all your soul and with all your might. (Deuteronomy 6:5)

There will be only two valuable pursuits in the lives of our children: to know God and to love Him. In the framework of their knowledge of God, a consuming love for Him will become the primary motivating force in their lives. The persons they will become will not flow out of their insights but out of their passions. As we studied earlier, our children's love for God will be developed in the context of their relationship with us as parents. As we give ourselves to them and stimulate a love response toward us, the same response of love can flow toward their Father in heaven. That love will then compel them in all of their lives and ministry.

> And these words that I command you today shall be on your heart. (Deuteronomy 6:6)

In preparation for a ministry of teaching children, we need to be reminded again that modeling will be the power behind all of our instruction. The words that God speaks must be "upon our hearts" if our teaching is to have authority and life. Because children are quick to see through hypocrisy, if we present to them a double standard, they will reject what we teach them.

THE MINISTRY OF THE WORD

> You shall teach them diligently to your children, and shall talk of them when you sit in your house, and when you walk by the way, and when you lie down, and when you rise. (Deuteronomy 6:7)

Moses gives us a wonderful picture of teaching the Scriptures to our children in the normal circumstances of life—when we gather together at home, when we are on our way from one place to another, when we lie down to rest, and when we arise to prepare for the day. The more we are able to relate the Word of God to real-life situations, the more effective our communication will be. The more we separate and remove the teaching of the Scriptures from our children's normal life experiences, the less effective it will be.

> You shall bind them as a sign on your hand, and they shall be as frontlets between your eyes. You shall write them on the doorposts of your house and on your gates. (Deuteronomy 6:8-9)

A home environment that is saturated with the words of God is a place in which children can grow in their perspective of His thoughts and ways. Our conversations, our wall plaques, our music and television can all be used to stimulate this environment. Our children will become comfortable with what they see and hear every day. We will want them to be comfortable with God rather than with the kingdom of this world.

> When your son asks you in time to come, "What is the meaning of the testimonies and the statutes and the rules that the LORD our God has commanded you?" then you shall say to your son, "We were Pharaoh's slaves in Egypt. And the LORD brought us out of Egypt with a mighty hand. And the LORD showed signs and wonders, great and grievous, against Egypt and against Pharaoh and all his household, before our eyes. (Deuteronomy 6:20-22)

Moses continues to give the people of God practical help in their ministry to their children. Children will ask about the things we teach and what we believe. These are opportunities to share about how God has met us, cared for us, and delivered us in a variety of situations.

> And he brought us out from there, that he might bring us in and give us the land that he swore to give to our fathers. And the LORD commanded us to do all these statutes, to fear the LORD our God, for our good always, that he might preserve us alive, as we are this day. And it will be righteousness for us, if we are careful to do all this commandment before the LORD our God, as he has commanded us. (Deuteronomy 6:23-25)

Since God has given children inquisitive minds, their questions provide natural teaching opportunities. Parents are then able to follow through effectively by giving their children God's mind and God's Word in these areas. This is the most effective time to give teaching concerning God, life, sex, relationships, finances, or any other area. When children ask questions, they are ready to receive answers.

Another effective teaching opportunity occurs when a child or young person is involved in a problem area. This might include conflicts within the home, conflicts with friends, the kinds of friends to choose, difficulties with discipline or motivation, purpose for the future, etc., and is the time for parents to give directive teaching from God's Word.

When children ask questions or when "problems" (opportunities to grow and learn) arise, the most effective teaching is from God's Word. The more a child can learn through his own study, the more effective the teaching will be. Though it will be necessary to spend time studying the Word together with young children as they mature in their understanding, you as parents will be able to work out a study project with some Scripture passages and say, "See what God's Word has to say about this." Set a time to get together again and share what the Scriptures say as well as what both of you have learned in the particular area.

Remember, let your children know you. It is seeing these things expressed personally and honestly in your experiences that cements them in your children's lives. Allow your children to spend time with you, watching you respond to people and situations with God's perspective and responses. These are often the most effective learning experiences. Your relationship with your children and their knowledge of you will be the environment in which they come to know God and in which their identity as His children are secured. Therefore, be free to reveal yourself fully to your children as God our Father does with us. Consistently share with them your thoughts and feelings, successes and failures, weaknesses and strengths, and the ways in which God has met you in the difficult times of your life as well as in your victories.

When my sons were in their teens, they felt that I had no idea at all what it meant to be a teenager in this world. Perhaps, in many ways, they were right. But I knew that I had already walked through many of the temptations and difficulties that they were dealing with. In some of those places, I experienced great failures. In some places, God gave me great victories. Am I willing to let my sons know me in those places? God has used those times of vulnerability not only to teach my sons but also to develop intimacy among us.

Naked & Unashamed

A NEW COVENANT

As we communicate to our children an understanding of who God is and what He is like, and as we seek to build into their hearts a love for Him that will become the primary motivating force in all of their lives, we must always come back to the heart of the Christian life. God has given us a new-covenant relationship with Him through His Son. The last night Jesus spent with His disciples before going to the cross, He took the cup and said,

> ..."This cup that is poured out for you is the new covenant in my blood." (Luke 22:20)

Through His death on the cross, Jesus brings a completely new relationship with the Father to all who would place their trust in Him. It is a relationship filled with forgiveness, life, freedom, righteousness and intimacy. It is also filled with great power. The apostle Paul describes this new life to the church at Corinth:

> Such is the confidence that we have through Christ toward God. Not that we are sufficient in ourselves to claim anything as coming from us, but our sufficiency is from God, who has made us competent to be ministers of a new covenant, not of the letter but of the Spirit. For the letter kills, but the Spirit gives life. (2 Corinthians 3:4-6)

Before we came to know Christ, all of the resources for our lives came from ourselves. We learned to trust in our own strength, our own wisdom, and our own ability to work things out, but in Christ, we put no confidence in ourselves. All of our adequacy, power, and sufficiency now come from Christ.

This is the truth we must continually give our children. In a world in which they will receive much training and excellent education and in which they will be developed as resource people, we must teach them every day to place their confidence in Christ. When they need wisdom, they must not trust in themselves; they must come to Him. In the midst of temptation, they must place no confidence in themselves but rather, run to Christ! If they have difficulties in relationships, rather than try to work it out on their own, they must place their hope and trust in God.

During the last hours Jesus spent with His disciples, He set this truth before them.

> I am the vine; you are the branches. Whoever abides in me and I in him, he it is that bears much fruit, for apart from me you can do nothing. (John 15:5)

As in the case of many families, our two sons, Peter and Joel, are vastly different from one another. They have different strengths and weaknesses, different needs and vulnerabilities. They have had excellent academic strengths and some real weaknesses. They have also brought special strengths to relationships and have experienced real shortcomings. However, we have seen that often their areas of strength have brought great vulnerability because of a tendency to trust in themselves and in their own abilities. Sometimes it is easier to teach them to trust in God when the needs are obvious.

It is that way with all of us. We see the places in our lives in which we really need God's help and the places we think we can pretty well handle on our own. But in reality, there are no places like that. Apart from Him, we can do nothing. We must always remind our children that Christ is the only hope in every area of their lives, relationships, and ministry.

Paul summarized this message in his own call as a servant of the church of the Lord Jesus:

> ...of which I became a minister according to the stewardship

from God that was given to me for you, to make the word of God fully known, the mystery hidden for ages and generations but now revealed to his saints. To them God chose to make known how great among the Gentiles are the riches of the glory of this mystery, which is Christ in you, the hope of glory. (Colossians 1:25-27)

MEMORIAL STONES

One of the most powerful means of teaching truth to children is by way of "memorial stones." When Israel crossed the Jordan River after God had miraculously cut off the waters before them, God spoke to Joshua:

> When all the nation had finished passing over the Jordan, the LORD said to Joshua, "Take twelve men from the people, from each tribe a man, and command them, saying, 'Take twelve stones from here out of the midst of the Jordan, from the very place where the priests' feet stood firmly, and bring them over with you and lay them down in the place where you lodge to-night.'" (Joshua 4:1-3)

Joshua followed through with God's command and spoke to the people:

> And Joshua said to them, "Pass on before the ark of the LORD your God into the midst of the Jordan, and take up each of you a stone upon his shoulder, according to the number of the tribes of the people of Israel, that this may be a sign among you. When your children ask in time to come, 'What do those stones mean to you?' then you shall tell them that the waters of the Jordan were cut off before the ark of the covenant of the LORD. When it passed over the Jordan, the waters of the Jordan were cut off. So these stones shall be to the people of Israel a memorial forever." (Joshua 4:5-7)

God wants us to have specific tools that will help us remember His intimate, sovereign, powerful involvements in our lives. It is valuable to keep something as a remembrance of these times so that when children see and ask what these things mean, we can explain God's sovereign care. These "memorial stones" will then become visual reminders that God is there during the times that we need Him, always making the difference in our lives.

Memorial stones could mark the times God has protected you and your family by His sovereign power, brought healing and deliverance into your lives as an expression of His grace and mercy, or provided for your needs in a special way. These "stones" could be expressed as a tree that you plant, a specific purchase for your home that would be a focal point of remembrance, or even a special ministry that you provide for another family. Anything that would serve as a visible reminder to you and your family of the Person of God and His wonderful work on your behalf would be a "memorial stone" in your lives.

Earlier in this study I mentioned the auto accident that was a time of great trial and testing for our family. God brought us through that experience as He brought physical healing and financial provision, as well as protection for our hearts. When God provided a new home for us just a few months afterward, we placed four stones in the shrubs that we planted in the front of our house. These stones stand as a visual reminder to us of our Father's sovereign care and protection for our family.

PREPARING THE HEART OF A GENERATION

God's purpose for ministry within the family is the development of the knowledge of Him and the passing on of His life for generations.

> Give ear, O my people, to my teaching; incline your ears to the words of my mouth! I will open my mouth in a parable; I will utter dark sayings from of old, things that we have heard and known,

195

that our fathers have told us. We will not hide them from their children, but tell to the coming generation the glorious deeds of the LORD, and his might, and the wonders that he has done. (Psalm 78:1-4)

In these verses, God reveals His purpose in giving us His Word: so that fathers and mothers might teach their children and so that the truth might pass from generation to generation. Our children develop confidence in God as they learn what He has done and the way in which He has powerfully intervened in their lives in time, space, and history. Most of all, God desires obedience and responsiveness to Him and His Word, in contrast to the rebellion and unfaithfulness that characterize the world now and in past generations.

He established a testimony in Jacob and appointed a law in Israel, which he commanded our fathers to teach to their children, that the next generation might know them, the children yet unborn, and arise and tell them to their children, so that they should set their hope in God and not forget the works of God, but keep his commandments; and that they should not be like their fathers, a stubborn and rebellious generation, a generation whose heart was not steadfast, whose spirit was not faithful to God. (Psalm 78:5-8)

One of the greatest questions facing the church today is, How do we prepare the hearts of a generation? God had spoken to His people Israel, calling them to obey Him, to praise His name, to tell of His works. The generation before them had not done this; it was a generation whose hearts had not been prepared. Our awesome responsibility and eternal stewardship from our Father in heaven is to prepare the hearts of the next generation so they will be faithful to God. God's Word makes clear to us how this ministry is fulfilled in our children: the revelation of the Person and the works of God, the development of a desire to know Him, and a heart that is responsive to Him in every way. In this way our children will learn to live for the praise of His glory.

We have a great challenge before us as we seek to prepare the hearts of this generation, which is the most self-confident and materialistic generation that has ever lived. Like no generation before, it is preparing to consume this world on itself and even feel right about it in the process. How do we open the eyes of our children to see what God sees?

Our sons have been children of their generation with a love for designer clothes and dreams of high-paying jobs and sport cars. One of the most powerful tools God has used to transform their hearts is their experience on the mission field. Traveling to the developing world and even our own inner cities can expose our children to the needs of the poor. Being involved with missions during our children's formative years lets them see what God is doing around the world.

It is through these experiences that God might grip the hearts of our children for the building of His Kingdom, whether they stay at home or physically go to the mission field. I strongly encourage you to get your children to the mission field during their teen years. Your church or denomination may offer opportunities, and many ministries specialize in these projects. Our children tend to be isolated from the real needs of people who are hurting. They must see and experience real needs and viable ministry opportunities. Otherwise, Satan may very well use the glories of this system to cause our children to consume this world on themselves.

UNLEASHING OUR CHILDREN

The psalmist gives us a very graphic picture of the ministry of parents:

> Behold, children are a heritage from the LORD, the fruit of the womb a reward. (Psalm 127:3)

Children are a gift from the Lord! They are a heritage that we receive and prepare. Our children are an inheritance for generations to come, for the church of the Lord Jesus, and for the Kingdom of God.

Like arrows in the hand of a warrior are the children of one's youth. (Psalm 127:4)

Just as arrows are aimed and released, so it is with our children. During the years that God entrusts them to us, we are shaping their ministry, their hearts, and their spirits with the love of God and the words He speaks. We are aiming our children and preparing to release them. At what are they aimed? For what purpose will we release them?

Blessed is the man who fills his quiver with them! He shall not be put to shame when he speaks with his enemies in the gate. (Psalm 127:5)

We are unleashing our children against the forces of darkness. Just as the psalmist described children contending with their enemies, so it is with our own children. We are preparing them to contend with their enemies and with the enemies of God. Our families are engaged in a great war. God is raising us up as vessels through which He will pour His life into this world and fill the earth with His glory. For that reason, Satan is seeking to destroy us and our children.

Aim your children at the forces of wickedness in the heavenly places. Prepare them for battle by your prayers, your modeling, and your teaching. Release them for the work of God's Kingdom; aim them; let them go for God's eternal purposes.

LIVING FOR THE GLORY OF GOD

The most important ministry parents will ever fulfill in the lives of their children is to give them something to live for that is worthy of their whole lives. Only one purpose is high enough to warrant the consummation of our lives: the glory of God. As we teach our children to live for God's glory—the same reason for which He lives—all of His will shall be fulfilled in their lives.

After God had provided His people Israel with a land of abundance and fullness of life under His care, they refused to enter because of unbelief. They saw giants in the land and were afraid. Rather than glory in an all-powerful, all-sufficient God, they focused on their own inadequacies and fears. God's anger burned against them, and Moses' interceded on their behalf before the Lord. In His mercy, God did forgive the people in response to Moses' prayer, but he follows his statement of forgiveness with an oath that none of those who were disobedient would enter the Promised Land.

But it is in the midst of the bad news God gives to the Israelites that the words that introduce His oath reveal His heart: "truly, as I live, and *as all the earth shall be filled with the glory of the LORD...*" (Numbers 14:20-21, emphasis added), and we see God's passion for His own glory.

God lives in order that all of His creation might be filled with His glory! His purpose, the reason for everything He does, the motive behind every act is His desire to glorify Himself. All of our lives must be brought in line with His will, and He will teach us to live for the same purpose for which He lives. God desires His glory to be our purpose in life, the reason for everything we do, the motive behind every act.

Our ministry to our children will be fulfilled as we teach them to live for the same purpose for which God lives—that everything of their lives (their words, thoughts, actions, feelings, priorities, motives, values, goals) would grow out of a desire to see God glorified. Only this goal is worthy of their lives. As we and our children learn to live as God lives, He will fulfill His will not only in our lives but in all of His creation, and generations will be raised up to give Him glory!

> In place of your fathers shall be your sons; you will make them princes in all the earth. I will cause your name to be remembered in all generations; therefore nations will praise you forever and ever. (Psalm 45:16-17)

GROUP STUDY GUIDE
AND PERSONAL APPLICATION

1. What does it mean to "train up a child in the way he should go?"

2. In teaching our children about God's attributes and His character, what kind of things will they learn about God?

3. Why must we be careful to not be hypocritical before our children?

4. In Deuteronomy 6:7 we find suggestions about when we can teach God's truths to our children. What does it say?

5. Children love to ask questions. How can we use their inquisitiveness as a teaching tool?

6. Explain the significance of the memorial stones the Lord instructed Joshua to set before the people of Israel.

7. What were the Israelites to tell their children about the stones?

8. How can we use memorial stones today?

9. According to Psalm 78:1-4, what are we to tell future generations?

10. How do our children learn to develop confidence in God?

11. Psalm 127:4 likens our children to arrows being aimed and released. Explain this comparison.

12. What should be our purpose in releasing our children?

13. At what should we "aim" our children and why?

REFLECTIONS

Teaching God's Word and daily modeling biblical truths go hand in hand. Much of what our children learn from us is not so much "taught" as "caught." That is, it is often in our day-to-day, hour-by-hour walk through life as we model our Christianity that our children learn what it means to live all of life as unto the Lord. Deuteronomy 6:8-9 encourages us to saturate our homes with reminders of God. List some tangible ways in which you can bring remembrances of God and His great works into your home. How can you help your children to become more comfortable with the things of God's kingdom rather than the kingdom of this world? Remember that when we give our children a way of life that comes from God, we share together with them as heirs of His life.

A TIME OF PRAYER

As we close this study, will you again submit your relationship to God? As we ask Him to build us into what He wants us to be, our marriages will become richer than we ever imagined. As we submit our dreams and goals to Him, He begins a growth process in our marriages that will last a lifetime. Below is a summary of the teaching you have received through this study. We urge you to use this list as a base and pray that God will build these things into your relationship.

• **God's desire for your marriage.** His character and His love are to be reflected to the world, and you will together become a vessel through which His glory fills the earth.

• **Shared dominion.** The command to rule was given to both husband and wife to be shared. How can we share more fully in our marriages?

• **A suitable helper.** The woman protects the man's heart and emotions, thus bringing him the ministry of God. The man must be open to the way in which he needs help and must allow the woman to be his helper.

• ***Naked and not ashamed.*** We must learn to accept one another just as we are and allow our marriage partners to see us as we really are.

• ***The effects of the curse.*** Men are affected in relation to their work. They tend to focus on their jobs and seek in them the satisfaction that only God can give. Women are affected in relation to their homes. They tend to center their thoughts and hopes on their families rather than on God. We need God to redeem these areas from the effects of the curse.

• ***Headship and submission.*** The only role in marriage is to serve one another. The husband gives himself up for his wife, and the spirit of a wife creates an environment in which her husband can grow into everything God wants him to be.

• ***Loving one another.*** We must take seriously our responsibilities to serve one another, to build up our spouses, and to put their interests before ours. This will lead us to bear burdens, to exhort and rebuke, and to encourage and support.

• ***Priorities.*** The priorities established in the Scriptures are clear: God, marriage, family, vocation and overflowing ministry, in that order. The problem arises not so much in knowing the right priority but in living it out by God's grace.

• ***Dealing with conflict.*** We must learn to respond to one another with love and forgiveness. We do not return evil for evil, but rather we seek to return a blessing.

• ***Disciplining children.*** This is the ministry of building into your children the right motivations, priorities, and values, and teaching them to channel who they are into fulfilling God's will. With the strength to endure, your children will be able to run the race of life in a way that glorifies God and not fall before the finish line.

• ***Teaching children.*** This involves developing within your children a knowledge of the person of God and teaching them to understand His thoughts, His ways, and His works. Knowing God will be the key to your children's lives, and stimulating within them the desire to know Him will be the most valuable inheritance you give to them.

Scripture Index

Leadership Resources International

If you have been encouraged by this book, you might consider using it in a small group or class in your church. You might also consider inviting Bill to teach the Bible conference "Recapturing Family Intimacy," which is based on this book, in your church.

Our desire is to magnify God in the eyes of His people so that they may stand in awe, wonder and worship before Him, and be transformed in His presence. We do this as we bring the encouragement of the Scriptures to churches, pastors and missions. The largest aspect of our work is encouraging and equipping pastors in the developing world who often have little formal training for the ministry. These ministries take place throughout Latin America, China, Burma, Russia and Africa. We invite your church to partner with us in one of these training times.

For more information about our conferences or materials, contact:

Leadership Resources
12575 South Ridgeland Avenue
Palos Heights, IL 60463
(800) 980–2226
www.leadershipresources.org